THE
CABINET-MAKER
& UPHOLSTERER'S
GUIDE

THE
CABINET-MAKER
& UPHOLSTERER'S
GUIDE

George Hepplewhite

THE THIRD EDITION OF 1794

WITH A NEW INTRODUCTION BY

JOSEPH ARONSON

DOVER PUBLICATIONS, INC., NEW YORK

Published in Canada by General Publishing Company, Ltd.,
30 Lesmill Road, Don Mills, Toronto, Ontario.
Published in the United Kingdom by Constable and Company, Ltd.,
10 Orange Street, London WC 2.

This Dover edition, first published in 1969, is an unabridged and
unaltered republication of the third (1794) edition, as published by
I. and J. Taylor, London. A new introduction has been written
specially for the present edition by Joseph Aronson.

Standard Book Number: 486-22183-0
Library of Congress Catalog Card Number: 69-19164

Manufactured in the United States of America
Dover Publications, Inc.
180 Varick Street
New York, N. Y. 10014

INTRODUCTION TO THE DOVER EDITION

The sole documented fact presently known about George Hepplewhite is that he died. This event in 1786 preceded by two years the first appearance of his monument, the publication entitled *The Cabinet-Maker and Upholsterer's Guide . . . from drawings*, over the name of A. Hepplewhite and Co. Cabinet-Makers, and published by I. and J. Taylor, "at the Architectural Library, No. 56, Holborn, opposite Great Turn-Stile" in London. The 1788 debut was followed the next year by a slightly revised edition, and in 1794 by the "improved" third edition which is reproduced here.

A. Hepplewhite, the widow Alice, was granted administration of the estate of George Hepplewhite on June 27, 1786. Described as "less than £600," this estate could hardly have been the residue of a wildly successful business, compared with the substantial contemporary enterprises of which records survive. Of his business, and of George Hepplewhite's personal life, there remains no attributable vestige: no stick of wood, no shred of paper, no bills or letters. The name appears in print only on six plates in a contemporary publication, *The Cabinet-Makers' London Book of Prices*, editions of 1788 and later. Twenty plates by Thomas Shearer and three by W. Casement which complete this work bear a strong family resemblance, as do all the plates of Shearer's *Designs for Household Furniture* (1788) and, to an extent, even some of Thomas Sheraton's examples in his 1791 *Drawing Book*. The inevitable question is, How did the name of George Hepplewhite come to identify a complete school of furniture design, the style of the whole generation after Chippendale's *Director*?

The broad answer is, of course, that there remains a book illustrating work of the period and bearing Hepplewhite's name. The architecture and allied arts of the eighteenth century were effectively memorialized in a significant library of contemporary origin.* Three works stand out by

---

* The most important publications to 1788 are the following:

1740	Batty Langley, *A Treasury of Designs*
1740	Matthias Lock, *A New Drawing Book of Ornaments*
1744	Matthias Lock, *Six Sconces*
1746	Matthias Lock, *Six Tables*
n.d.	Matthias Lock, *A book of Ornaments . . . principally adapted for carvers*

reason of their comprehensive scope, the quality of their engravings, the definiteness of their subject matter in delineating a style-period, and their wide distribution at home and abroad. Chippendale, Hepplewhite, and Sheraton are the trisyllabic triad who throughout the nineteenth century were credited with the total furniture output of the Georgian era. In the early decades of the twentieth century serious researchers—Constance Simon, R. S. Clouston, Percy Macquoid, Ralph Edwards, Margaret Jourdain, and Herbert Cescinsky, among others—compared bills and labels, account books and letters, drawings and actual surviving furniture. Their conclusions, paired with careful reading of texts, and dedicatory remarks in particular, call for a reappraisal of the functions and motivations of the three immortal masters. In short, these men live through their publications rather than through their furniture performances.

The Preface to the Hepplewhite work is a treasury of inferences. As modest as it is brief, it neither implies originality nor imputes design invention to Hepplewhite. It is directed first to the artisan, secondly to the gentleman; it has no list of patrons or subscribers, although such lists were usual in publications of the period. It clearly states its intention of depicting only accepted designs, eschewing "mere novelty, . . . whim at the instance of caprice" and adhering to "such articles only as are of general use and service" for the guidance of "Foreigners, who seek a knowledge of English taste" as well as "Cou[n]trymen and Artizans" distant from the metropolis. The inference that may be drawn from this is that Widow Alice had the enterprise to make capital of her inheritance of accumulated drawings, sketches, memory-aids, and possibly models, of the late George's furniture notes and/or ideas.

A second inference is that Alice collated the efforts and ideas of contemporaries like Thomas Shearer, whose style is indistinguishable from Hepplewhite's. With many more examples extant to judge by, Shearer's drawings bespeak, by their very differences, the same hand trying to be different. A conspicuous example is the unsigned Plate 79 in the *Guide*, Rudd's Table, and Rudd's Table, Plate 4, signed "Thos. Shearer del,

1750 and after	William and John Halfpenny (son), at least 12 publications, primarily architecture on Chinese motifs, but with some chairs, etc.
1752 to 1768	Matthias Lock and Henry Copeland, *A New Book of Ornaments, Consisting of Tables, Chimnies, Sconces . . .*
1754 (1755, 1762)	Thomas Chippendale, *The Gentleman and Cabinet-Maker's Director*
1757	Sir William Chambers, *Designs of Chinese Buildings, Furniture, . . .*
1758	Thomas Johnson, *One Hundred and Fifty New Designs*
1759–1763	William Ince and John Mayhew, *The Universal System of Household Furniture* (based on the *Director;* printed in English and French)
1760	The Society of Upholsterers and Cabinet-makers, *Household Furniture in Genteel Taste* (Chippendale, Ince and Mayhew, and Johnson contributed)
1765	Robert Manwaring, *The Cabinet and Chair Makers' Real Friend and Companion*
1766	Robert Manwaring, *The Chair-makers' Guide*
1774	Robert Adam, *Works in Architecture*
1788	Thomas Shearer, *Designs for Household Furniture, The Cabinet-Makers' London Book of Prices*

1788," in the 1793 edition of *The Cabinet-Makers' London Book of Prices*. Perspective, handles, graining are different, but the concept, parts, and proportions are identical.

Speculation is further invited by the differences between the 1788 and the 1794 editions of the *Guide*, changes that were undoubtedly prompted by the belittling criticism of the Hepplewhite book in Sheraton's 1791 *Drawing Book*. Hepplewhite had certainly mastered the Rococo, absorbing rather than adopting the foreign influence. Cabriole legs, and in fact the whole Louis Quinze vocabulary, appear until almost 1790 in tasteful relation to more Adamesque details; the style is clearly Anglicized, and the transition to Louis Seize influences is gradual and graceful. The cabriole leg is sculpture, not truly rendered in any convention of drawing. It appears in the first edition of the *Guide* in various adaptations in chairs and sofas. These pieces are entirely deleted from the 1794 issue, except for two stools, Plates 16 and 17, and a Pier Table, Plate 65, the latter sagging on cabriole legs equal to the worst Settecento Italian. (The title "Cabriole Chairs" on Plates 10 and 11 conveys an out-of-date specialized use of the word, which has no relation to "cabriole" as a leg shape.) Replacing the French-inspired designs are two pages of poorly drawn, weakly engraved post-1790 square-back chairs, blatantly lacking the Hepplewhite feel.

Another open field of conjecture is Hepplewhite's association with the Adams and with other cabinetmakers like Gillow. The Adelphi diverted Gothic and Rococo and Chinese eclecticism of the Chippendale generation toward their own Classicism. Every known cabinetmaker employed classic Roman formality and ornamentation after 1760, whether or not he worked for the Adams. Robert Adam was a great architect and designer, a casual decorator, but at best an off-hand designer of furniture, lacking conspicuously a sense of material. George Hepplewhite, intuitively sensitive to material and a disciplined craftsman, may well have taken Adam's direction as to form and proportion and made the designs constructible in wood. The lacy drips and festoons, effected in compo glued to wires, must have offended him; they appear sparingly in Hepplewhite's patterns, but the motives occur constantly in inlays, appliqués of carved wood or compo, and most originally in painted form. If Hepplewhite did not actually execute some of Robert Adam's commissions, or even delineate them for the cabinetmaker, he may have recorded these designs either as draftsman or merely observer. Such sketches may well have been the bulk of the widow's property.

Such deduction considers the possibility that Hepplewhite was a designer or delineator divorced from the craftsman. This occupation was the end product of the evolution from cottage handicraft through the Factory System and the Industrial Revolution. The eighteenth century saw the ultimate division of functions in the crafts, aiming for greater output and efficiency to meet the demands of expanding markets and wealth. The designer filled a place similar to that of the sawyer, joiner, turner, carver, and others. In modern practice, the classic book drawings would be considered mere sketches, wholly inadequate for production patterns, lacking precise dimensions and details. So it may be assumed that the training of the specialized craftsman had attained such perfection that competence meant knowing to a hair the proper thickness and taper of a leg, the depth of carving, the provision for jointing. The sum of the skills of the British furniture industry of Hepplewhite's era is unsurpassed in other times and places. The fact remains that surviving furniture of the period, especially the so-called book furniture, is always better than its representation: witness the weak bases of the commodes and chests in Plates 76, 77, and 78; the over-thin show-wood framings of shield-back chairs; the coarseness of some tapered legs and chest members.

Employment of such detached designers is suggested in surviving records, letters, and cost-books of the larger organizations of the period—Gillow, Seddon, Vile and Cobb, Linnell, Hallett, and others. Possibly a man like Hepplewhite guided a design through the critical progress from sketch to refined actuality. There is a tenuous, folklorish association between Hepplewhite and the Gillows, beginning with his supposed origin in Lancashire, a furniture center where the Gillow firm was established in the early decades of the century; Hepplewhite's rumored apprenticeship there; Gillow's establishment of a branch in Oxford street, London, a few years after Hepplewhite's shop is noted in Redcross street, Cripplegate. Furniture marked "Gillow, Lancaster" is remarkably close to some of the *Guide* drawings, as are sketches in the well-kept Gillow cost-books. But since this is equally true of some Sheraton drawings, the threads of identification become further tangled rather than unraveled by research into Gillow and other contemporaries.*

For all the ambiguity of its origins, the *Guide* is no less successful as a summary of a style, since it proved to be valuable as a guide to far-flung Englishmen and to Europe as a whole. As a compilation or anthology it succeeds admirably in the purpose stated in the Preface. If art is selection, the choice and scope of the examples is an act of artistic creativity. The style of the generation 1760–1790 is well named the school of Hepplewhite.

Halcott Center, New York   JOSEPH ARONSON
January, 1969

---

* "If Richard Gillow had thought it worth his while to publish a book of designs about the same time as Hepplewhite produced the *Guide* there might well be two opinions as to whose name we should now use in describing the style," Cescinsky, *English Furniture of the Eighteenth Century.*

IMPORTANT MODERN STUDIES
OF THE HEPPLEWHITE PERIOD

Bell, J. M., *Furniture Designs of George Hepplewhite*, 1910.

Blake, J. P., and Reviers-Hopkins, A. E., *Little Books about Old Furniture*, 1911.

Cescinsky, Herbert, *English Furniture of the Eighteenth Century*, 1910; *English Furniture from Gothic to Sheraton*, 1929, 1937 (Dover reprint, 1968).

Clouston, R. S., *English Furniture and Furniture Makers of the Eighteenth Century*, 1906.

Edwards, Ralph, and Jourdain, Margaret, *Georgian Cabinetmakers*, 1944, 1955.

Heal, Sir Ambrose, *The London Furniture Makers from the Restoration to the Victorian Era*, 1953.

Hunter, George Leland, *Decorative Furniture*, 1923.

Macquoid, Percy, *History of English Furniture* (4 vols.), 1904–1908.

Macquoid, Percy, and Edwards, Ralph, *The Dictionary of English Furniture* (3 vols.), 1924.

Musgrave, Clifford, *Adam and Hepplewhite*, 1966.

THE
CABINET-MAKER
AND
UPHOLSTERER's GUIDE;
OR,
REPOSITORY OF DESIGNS
FOR EVERY ARTICLE OF
HOUSEHOLD FURNITURE,
IN THE NEWEST AND MOST APPROVED TASTE:
DISPLAYING
A GREAT VARIETY OF PATTERNS FOR

Chairs	Tea Caddies	Hanging Shelves
Stools	Tea Trays	Fire Screens
Sofas	Card Tables	Beds
Confidante	Pier Tables	Field Beds
Duchesse	Pembroke Tables	Sweep Tops for Ditto
Side Boards	Tambour Tables	Bed Pillars
Pedestals and Vases	Dressing Glasses	Candle Stands
Cellerets	Dressing Tables and Drawers	Lamps
Knife-Cases	Commodes	Pier Glasses
Desk and Book-Cases	Rudd's Table	Terms for Busts
Secretary and Book-Cases	Bidets	Cornices for Library
Library Cases	Night Tables	Cases, Wardrobes, &c. at large
Library Tables	Bason Stands	Ornamented Tops for Pier
Reading Desks	Wardrobes	Tables, Pembroke Tables,
Chests of Drawers	Pot Cupboards	Commodes, &c. &c.
Urn Stands	Brackets	

In the PLAINEST and most ENRICHED STYLES; with a SCALE to each, and an EXPLANATION in LETTER PRESS.

ALSO

THE PLAN OF A ROOM,
SHEWING THE PROPER DISTRIBUTION OF THE FURNITURE.

The Whole exhibiting near THREE HUNDRED different DESIGNS, engraved on ONE HUNDRED and TWENTY-EIGHT PLATES:

FROM DRAWINGS

By A. HEPPLEWHITE and Co. CABINET-MAKERS.

THE THIRD EDITION, IMPROVED.

LONDON:
Published by I. and J. TAYLOR, at the ARCHITECTURAL LIBRARY,
No. 56, HOLBORN, opposite GREAT TURN-STILE.
MDCCXCIV.

P R E F A C E.

TO unite elegance and utility, and blend the useful with the agreeable, has ever been considered a difficult, but an honourable task. How far we have succeeded in the following work it becomes not us to say, but rather to leave it, with all due deference, to the determination of the Public at large.

It may be allowable to say, we have exerted our utmost endeavours to produce a work which shall be useful to the mechanic, and serviceable to the gentleman. With this view, after having fixed upon such articles as were necessary to a complete suit of furniture, our judgment was called forth in selecting such patterns as were most likely to be of general use—in choosing such points of view as would shew them most distinctly—and in exhibiting such fashions as were necessary to answer the end proposed, and convey a just idea of English taste in furniture for houses.

English taste and workmanship have, of late years, been much sought for by surrounding nations; and the mutibility of all things, but more especially of fashions, has rendered the labours of our predecessors in this line of little use: nay, at this day, they can only tend to mislead those Foreigners, who seek a knowledge of English taste in the various articles of household furniture.

The same reason, in favour of this work, will apply also to many of our own Courtrymen and Artizans, whose distance from the metropolis makes even an imperfect knowledge of its improvements acquired with much trouble and expence. Our labours will, we hope,

tend

PREFACE.

tend to remove this difficulty; and as our idea of the useful was such articles as are generally serviceable in genteel life, we flatter ourselves the labour and pains we have bestowed on this work will not be considered as time uselessly spent.

To Residents in London, though our drawings are all new, yet, as we designedly followed the latest or most prevailing fashion only, purposely omitting such articles, whose recommendation was mere novelty, and perhaps a violation of all established rule, the production of whim at the instance of caprice, whose appetite must ever suffer disappointment if any similar thing had been previously thought of; we say, having regularly avoided those fancies, and steadily adhered to such articles only as are of general use and service, one principal hope for favour and encouragement will be, in having combined near three hundred different patterns for furniture in so small a space, and at so small a price. In this instance we hope for reward; and though we lay no claim to extraordinary merit in our designs, we flatter ourselves they will be found serviceable to young workmen in general, and occasionally to more experienced ones.

INDEX

TO

ARTICLES.

INDEX.

THE

CABINET-MAKER

AND

UPHOLSTERER's GUIDE, &c.

CHAIRS.

THE general dimenſion and proportion of chairs are as follow: Width in front 20 inches, depth of the ſeat 17 inches, height of the ſeat frame 17 inches; total height about 3 feet 1 inch.

Other dimenſions are frequently adapted according to the ſize of the room, or pleaſure of the purchaſer.

Chairs in general are made of mahogany, with the bars and frame funk in a hollow, or rifing in a round projection, with a band or lift on the inner and outer edges. Many of thefe defigns are enriched with ornaments proper to be carved in mahogany as the defigns A B, plates 1, 2, &c.

Mahogany chairs fhould have the feats of horfe hair, plain, ftriped, checquered, &c. at pleafure, or cane bottoms with cufhions, the cafes of which fhould be covered with the fame as the curtains.

For chairs, a new and very elegant fafhion has arifen within thefe few years, of finifhing them with painted or japanned work, which gives a rich and fplendid appearance to the minuter parts of the ornaments, which are generally thrown in by the painter. Several of thefe defigns are particularly adapted to this ftyle, which allows a frame-work lefs maffy than is requifite for mahogany; and by afforting the prevailing colour to the furniture and light of the room, affords opportunity, by the variety of grounds which may be introduced, to make the whole accord in harmony, with a pleafing and ftriking effect to the eye. Japanned chairs fhould have cane bottoms, with linen or cotton cafes over cufhions to accord with the general hue of the chair.

Plate 9.* Two defigns for chairs with cane bottoms; thefe may be of mahogany or japanned, and fhould have cufhions of linen, leather, &c.

CHAIRS WITH STUFFED BACKS

ARE called cabriole chairs. The defigns E F plate 10 are of the neweft fafhion; the arms to F, though much higher than ufual, have

been

been executed with good effect for his Royal Highnefs the Prince of Wales.   The defigns, plate 11, are alfo quite new.

Plate 12, 13, exhibit twelve defigns for chair backs, proper to be executed in mahogany or japan; fome of them applicable to the more elegant kind of chairs with backs and feats of red or blue morocco leather, in thefe backs which are fometimes made a little circular, are frequently inferted medallions, printed or painted on filk of the natural colours; when the backs and feats are of leather they fhould be tied down with taffels of filk or thread as fhewn in feveral of the preceding defigns.

HALL CHAIRS.

PLATE 14 fhews three defigns for hall chairs, which are made all of wood, either carved or painted.   The defigns with vafe backs are new, and have been much approved.

Plate 15 fhews a defign for a *Saddle Check*, or eafy chair; the conftruction and ufe of which is very apparent: they may be covered with leather, horfe-hair; or have a linen cafe to fit over the canvafs ftuffing as is moft ufual and convenient.

On the fame plate is fhewn the mechanifm of a *Gouty Stool*; the conftruction of which, by being fo eafily raifed or lowered at either end, is particularly ufeful to the afflicted.

STOOLS.

S T O O L S.

PLATES 16, 17, fhew four defigns for ftools; the frame-work for which may be of mahogany, or japanned, as moft agreeable; or to match the fuit of chairs, and of confequence fhould have the fame fort of covering. The defign O, plate 17, is proper for a dreffing or mufic ftool.

W I N D O W   S T O O L S.

TWO defigns are fhewn on plate 18, proper for mahogany or ja-pan, covered with linen or cotton to match the chairs. Plate 19, two more defigns; the upper one is applicable to japan-work, with ftriped furniture; the under one of mahogany, carved, with furniture of an elegant pattern feftooned in front, will produce a very pleafing ef-fect. Plate 20. Thefe two defigns are peculiarly adapted for an elegant drawing-room of japanned furniture; the covering fhould be of taberray or morine, of a pea-green, or other light colour.

The fize of window ftools muft be regulated by the fize of the place where they are to ftand; their heights fhould not exceed the feats of the chairs.

S O F A S.

PLATES 21, 22, 23, 24, prefent four defigns for fofas; the wood-work of which fhould be either mahogany or japanned, in accordance to the chairs; the covering alfo muft be of the fame.

The dimenfions of fofas vary according to the fize of the room and pleafure of the purchafer. The following is the proportion in gene-

ral

ral use : length between 6 and 7 feet, depth about 30 inches, height of the seat frame 14 inches ; total height in the back 3 feet 1 inch.

Plate 25 shews a design for a sofa of the newest fashion ; the frame should be japanned, with green on a white ground, and the edges gilt ; the covering of red Morocco leather.

Plate 26 is a design for a bar-back sofa : this kind of sofa is of modern invention ; and the lightness of its appearance has procured it a favourable reception in the first circles of fashion. The pattern of the back must match the chairs ; these also will regulate the sort of frame-work and covering.

CONFIDANTE.

THIS piece of furniture is of French origin, and is in pretty general request for large and spacious suits of apartments. An elegant drawing-room with modern furniture, is scarce complete without a confidante : the extent of which may be about 9 feet, subject to the same regulations as sofas. This piece of furniture is sometimes so constructed that the ends take away and leave a regular sofa : the ends may be used as Barjier chairs.

DUCHESSE.

This piece of furniture also is derived from the French. Two Barjier chairs, of proper construction, with a stool in the middle, form the duchesse, which is allotted to large and spacious anti-rooms : the covering may be various, as also the frame-work, and made from 6 to 8 feet long.

The

The ftuffing may be of the round manner as fhewn in the drawing or low-ftuffed, with a loofe fquab or bordered cufhion fitted to each part; with a duplicate linen cover to cover the whole, or each part feparately. Confidantes, Sofas, and Chairs may be ftuffed in the fame manner.

SIDEBOARDS.

THE great utility of this piece of furniture has procured it a very general reception; and the conveniencies it affords render a dining-room incomplete without a fideboard. Of thofe with drawers, we have given two defigns; the firft, on plate 29, fhews the internal con-ftruction and conveniencies of the drawers; the right hand drawer has partitions for nine bottles, as fhewn in the plan; the partition is one inch and a half from the bottom; behind this is a place for cloths or napkins the whole depth of the drawer.

The drawer on the left hand has two divifions, the hinder one lined with green cloth to hold plate, &c. under a cover; the front one is lined with lead for the convenience of holding water to wafh glaffes, &c.---there muft be a valve-cock or plug at the bottom, to let off the dirty water; and alfo in the other drawer, to change the water necef-fary to keep the wine, &c. cool; or they may be made to take out. The long drawer in the middle is adapted for table linen, &c.

Plate 30 fhews a different defign on the fame conftruction.

They are often made to fit into a recefs; but the general cuftom is to make them from 5 and a half to 7 feet long, 3 feet high, from 28 to 32 inches wide.

Plates

Plates 31, 32, 33, 34, are designs for sideboards without drawers; the ornaments to the fronts of which may be carved, painted, or inlaid with various coloured woods.

PEDESTALS AND VASES

ARE much used in spacious dining-rooms, where the last-described kind of sideboards are chosen; at each end of which they are placed. One pedestal serves as a plate-warmer, being provided with racks and a stand for a heater; and is lined with strong tin; the other pedestal is used as a pot cupboard.

The vases may be used to hold water for the use of the butler, or iced water for drinking, which is inclosed in an inner partition, the ice surrounding it; or may be used as knife-cases (see plate 39), in which case they are made of wood, carved, painted, or inlaid; if used for water may be made of wood or of copper japanned. The height of the pedestal is the same as the sideboard, and 16 or 18 inches square; the height of the vase about 2 feet 3 inches.

CELLERETS,

CALLED also *gardes de vin*, are generally made of mahogany, and hooped with brass hoops lacquered; the inner part is divided with partitions, and lined with lead for bottles; may be made of any shape. These are of general use where sideboards are without drawers; the proportion may be known by applying the scale.

KNIFE-

KNIFE-CASES.

THE univerfal utility of this piece of furniture renders a particular defcription not neceffary. Thofe on plate 38 may be made of mahogany inlaid, or of fatin, or other wood at pleafure.

Four defigns for *Vafe knife-cafes* are given on plate 39: they are ufually made of fatin or other light-coloured wood, and may be placed at each end on the fideboards, or on a pedeftal; the knives, &c. fall into the body of the vafe, the top of which is kept up by a fmall fpring which is fixed to the ftem which fupports the top; may be made of copper, painted and japanned.

DESK AND BOOK-CASE.

THIS article of furniture affords a great variety of patterns. The three defigns here given will fhew their general appearance.

Defks and book-cafes are ufually made of good mahogany; the drawers and internal conveniencies admit of much variation. The defigns fhew three different ways of making them: the patterns of the book-cafe doors may alfo be very much varied. On plate 40 are fhewn four defigns for doors, which will apply to any of the following defigns. On the top, when ornamented, is placed between a fcroll of foliage, a vafe, buft, or other ornament, which may be of mahogany, or gilt, or of light-coloured wood.

The dimenfions of this article, will in general, be regulated by the height of the room, the place where it muft ftand, or the particular ufe to which it is deftined. The following are the general proportions;

tions; length 3 feet 6 inches, depth 22 inches, height of defk 3 feet 2 inches, including 10 inches for the infide of the defk; total height about fix feet; depth of Book-cafe about 12 inches.

SECRETARY AND BOOK-CASES

HAVE the fame general ufe as the former article; they differ in not being floped in front. The accommodations therefore for writing are produced by the face of the upper drawer falling down by means of a fpring and quadrant, which produces the fame ufefulnefs as the flap to a defk. To one defign are drawers---the other has doors, within which are fliding fhelves for clothes, &c. like a wardrobe.

LIBRARY CASES.

PLATES 45, 46, 47, 48, fhew four different defigns for Library-cafes, which are ufually made of the fineft mahogany; the doors of fine waved or curled wood. May be inlaid on the pannels, &c. with various coloured woods. The ornamental fafh bars are intended to be of metal, which painted of a light colour, or gilt, will produce a light pleafing effect.

To each of thefe defigns, the drawer in the middle is intended for a fecretary drawer, with wardrobe fhelves under.

Various proper defigns at large, for *Cornices*, *Plinths*, and *Bafe Mouldings*, for this and the two former articles, are given at the end of this book.

The

The dimenſions of this article will depend entirely upon the place where it muſt ſtand.

L I B R A R Y　T A B L E S.

THREE deſigns are given on Plates 49, 50, for Library Tables, which are generally made of mahogany, covered on the top with leather or green cloth. Plate 49 ſhews a front with cupboards for books, papers, &c. ; the other ſide has drawers which run half-way back ; the dimenſions in uſe are from 3 to 4 feet long, by 3 feet deep.

R E A D I N G　D E S K S.

PLATE 51 ſhews two different kinds of Reading Deſks ; the mechaniſm and uſe of which are clearly ſhewn in the drawings. The deſk may be raiſed by means of the ſtaff which ſlides in the ſtem, and is fixed by the ſcrew at the top.

D R A W E R S.

Cheſts of Drawers. Two deſigns are here ſhewn for this article, which admits of little variation or ornament ; general dimenſions 3 feet 6 inches long, by 20 inches deep.

Double Cheſts of Drawers. Two deſigns for theſe are here ſhewn ; to the latter one is given fluted pilaſters at the angles ; theſe may have the ſame depth as the former ones, and height 5 feet 6 inches.

U R N

URN STANDS.

SIX defigns for this article are here fhewn, with their plans and proper enrichments, which may be inlaid of various coloured woods, or painted and varnifhed. The black line on the plan marks the flide, which draws out to fet the tea-pot on; their height may be about 26 inches.

TEA-CHESTS AND CADDIES.

FOR thefe articles fix defigns are here fhewn, with their plans. The ornaments may be inlaid with various coloured woods, or painted and varnifhed.

TEA TRAYS.

FOR Tea Trays a very great variety of patterns may be invented; almoft any kind of ornament may be introduced. Several very good and proper defigns may be chofen from the various kind of inlaid table tops which are given in this book. Four defigns for this article are here fhewn with the inner borders. Tea Trays may be inlaid of various coloured woods, or painted and varnifhed. This is an article where much tafte and fancy may be fhewn.

TABLES.

TABLES are of various kinds, adapted to the feveral ufes for which they are intended: in general, Tables are made of the beft mahogany. Their fize very various; but their height fhould not exceed 28 inches.

Card

Card Tables may be either fquare, circular or oval: the inner part is lined with green cloth; the fronts may be enriched with inlaid or painted ornaments; the tops alfo admit of great elegance in the fame ftyles. Plate 61 fhews four defigns proper for inlaid or painted *tops* for Card Tables.

Pembroke Tables are the moft ufeful of this fpecies of furniture: they may be of various fhapes. The long fquare and oval are the moft fafhionable. Thefe articles admit of confiderable elegance in the workmanfhip and ornaments. The defigns on Plate 63 are proper for *tops*, inlaid, or painted and varnifhed.

Pier Tables are become an article of much fafhion; and not being applied to fuch general ufe as other Tables, admit, with great propriety, of much elegance and ornament. Four defigns for Pier Tables are fhewn, with their proper ornaments; and alfo four defigns for *tops*, which fhew as many various plans.

The height of *Pier Tables* varies from the general rule, as they are now univerfally made to fit the pier, and rife level with or above the dado of the room, nearly touching the ornaments of the glafs: if the latter, the top fits clofe to the wall.

Tambour Writing Table is a very convenient piece of furniture, anfwering all the ufes of a defk, with a much lighter appearance. Plate 67 fhews a defign with two drawers, and the reids thrown back. Plate 68 is another defign, with four long drawers, with a flide to write on: the flap in which lifts up, and may be adjufted to any height by means of the foot or ftop behind.

Plate

Plate 69 ſhews a deſign for one with a *book-caſe* on it; the doors to which are intended to be made of, and ornamented with, metal frames; theſe painted of a light, or various colours, produce a lively and pleaſing effect.   The reeds are here drawn forward to ſhew the appearance when ſhut.

DRESSING APPARATUS.

Dreſſing Glaſſes.   Four deſigns are here ſhewn of different plans; the ornaments to which may be inlaid with various coloured woods, or painted and varniſhed.

Ladies' Dreſſing Tables.   Four deſigns, of various conſtructions and conveniencies, are here ſhewn; the partitions or apartments in which are adapted for combs, powders, eſſences, pin-cuſhions, and other neceſſary equipage.   The glaſſes riſe on hinges in the front, and are ſupported by a foot, affixed in the back; may be made of mahogany or other inferior wood.

Dreſſing Drawers.   Plate 74 ſhews a deſign for this article; the top drawer in which contains the neceſſary dreſſing equipage; the others are applicable to common uſes.

Plate 75 is a deſign for one with a ſlide.   Plate 76 ſhews two more deſigns, of different forms, in the fronts.

Plate 77 is a deſign for one with a *ſerpentine front*; the drawers to which are elegantly ornamented with inlaid or painted work, which is applied with great beauty and elegance to this piece of furniture.

Some

Some made of fatin wood, with the ornaments of fuitable colours, have produced a moft pleafing and agreeable effect.

Plate 78. Defign for a *Commode,* enriched with painted or inlaid work. This piece of furniture is adapted for a drawing-room; within are fhelves which anfwer the ufe of a clofet or cupboard--- may have one principal door in the front, or one at each end; are made of various fhapes; and being ufed in principal rooms, require confiderable elegance. The pannels may be of fatin wood, plain, or inlaid; the top and alfo the border round the front, fhould be inlaid.

The tops to thefe two laft articles are frequently inriched with inlaid or painted work: three defigns for which are here given on Plate 78*.

Rudd's Table, or *Reflecting Dreffing Table.* This is the moft complete dreffing table made, poffeffing every convenience which can be wanted, or mechanifm and ingenuity fupply. It derives its name from a once popular character, for whom it is reported it was firft invented. The middle drawer of this table flides by itfelf---the two end drawers are framed to the flide A, and faften at the catch B; and when difengaged, each drawer fwings horizontally on a centre pin at C, and may be placed in any ftation as fhewn in the drawing. The glaffes turn upward, and are fupported by a fpring at the bottom of the quadrant, which pufhed in, they fall down and flide under with the two end drawers. They alfo fwing on the pins D D. E is a flide co-

vered

vered with green cloth for writing on; F the bolt of the lock, which shoots into the lower rail.

Shaving Tables.   Two different kinds are here shewn; the tops of which turn over on each side; the glafs to each draws up in the back, and is supported by a spring stop; the situation of the glafs is regulated by a foot in the back; within the doors is a place for water bottles, &c.   The drawer is designed to hold napkins, &c.; are made of mahogany.

Plate 81 presents a *Dreffing* or *Shaving Table*, with the ufual conveniencies; and also a *Bidet*, which draws out and is supported by half-legs: this is on a new conftruction, and has been much approved for its ufe and conveniencies.

The glafs to this or other fimilar piece of furniture may be made with the face to turn inwards by means of a groove on each side, in which runs a pin fixed to the top of the glafs, which, if run up the grooves, will throw the face of the glafs outwards.   A foot may be fixed in the top of the table to regulate the fituation of the glafs.

Night Tables.   Plate 81 shews a design for one, with a tambour front; the feat of which draws out, and is supported by half-legs: Two more defigns are given on Plate 82 of different conftructions.

Bidet   Plate 83 shews the form of a common Bidet.

Bafon Stands.   A defign for a new one, Plate 83, on a triangular plan.   This is a very ufeful shape, as it stands in a corner out of the way.

Plate

Plate 84 shews three designs for Bason-stands of different construc-tions and various conveniencies.

WARDROBES.

THIS is an article of considerable consequence, as the conveni-encies experienced in their use make them a necessary piece of furni-ture; they are usually made plain, but of the best mahogany. Plate 85 shews a design with three drawers. Plate 86. Here the doors are shewn open, by which means the form and conveniencies of the slid-ing-shelves are plainly discovered. Plates 87, 88, shew a variation in two more designs. The dimensions may be 4 feet long, 22 inches deep, 5 feet 6 inches high or more.

POT-CUPBOARDS.

THREE designs are here shewn for pot-cupboards; an article of much use in bed-chambers, counting-houses, offices, &c.: the door in front swings on hinges at the side.

BRACKETS.

FOR Brackets here are six designs on Plates 90, 91. The open form of the three first, marked A, is particularly applicable to place lights on. Some of very large dimensions (6 or 7 feet high) have been made in this manner, for placing patent lamps on in the large sub-scription room at Newmarket: these should be of burnished gold. The three on Plate 91 are better calculated for clocks, Busts, &c. These may be of mahogany or gilt.

HANGING

HANGING SHELVES.

TWO defigns, with different patterns for fret-work, are given. Thefe are often wanted as *Book-fhelves* in clofets or Ladies' rooms: they alfo are adapted to place *China* on ; fhould be made of mahogany.

FIRE-SCREENS.

Pole Fire Screens are here reprefented in three defigns on Plate 93. The Screens may be ornamented varioufly, with maps, Chinefe figures, needle-work, &c. The fcreen is fufpended on the pole by means of a fpring in the eye, through which the pole goes; the feet of the two outer ones are loaded with lead to keep them fteady, may be made of mahogany, but more frequently of wood japanned.

Horfe Fire Screens. The frame-work to thefe fhould be of mahogany ; the fcreen may be covered with green filk, needle-work, &c. at pleafure. The fcreen flides in grooves in the inner fide of the uprights, and is fufpended by the weights, which are fhewn on the outfide ; and are connected to the fcreen by a line which paffes over a pulley in the top of the frame.

The fcreen to the fecond defign is fufpended by a weight at the end of the ribbon, which runs over the top bar on one fide.

BEDS.

ARE an article of much importance, as well on account of the great expence attending them, as the variety of fhapes, and the high degree of elegance which may be fhewn in them.

They

They may be executed of almoſt every ſtuff which the loom pro-duces.   White dimity, plain or corded, is peculiarly applicable for the furniture, which, with a fringe with a gymp head, produces an effect of elegance and neatneſs truly agreeable.

The Mancheſter ſtuffs have been wrought into Bed-furniture with good ſucceſs.   Printed cottons and linens are alſo very ſuitable ; the elegance and variety of patterns of which, afford as much ſcope for taſte, elegance, and ſimplicity, as the moſt lively fancy can wiſh. In general, the lining to theſe kinds of furniture is a plain white cot-ton.   To furniture of a dark pattern, a green ſilk lining may be uſed with a good effect.   From the deſigns, Plate 98, we have been informed, a bed, with little variation, has been made of dove-colourɔp ſatin curtains, with a lining of green ſilk.

In ſtate-rooms, where a high degree of elegance and grandeur are wanted, beds are frequently made of ſilk or ſatin, figured or plain, alſo of velvet, with gold fringe, &c.

The *Vallance* to elegant beds ſhould always be gathered full, which is called a *Petticoat Vallance*.   The *Cornices* may be either of maho-gany carved, carved and gilt, or painted and japanned.   The *Orna-ments* over the cornices may be in the ſame manner ; carved and gilt, or japanned, will produce the moſt lively effect.

Arms, or other ornaments to *Stuffed Head Boards*, ſhould be carved in ſmall relief, gilt and burniſhed.   The *Pillars* ſhould be of of maho-gany, with the enrichments carved.

Plate 95.   Deſign for a Bed.   The Vallance to this bed is tied up

in

in feftoons. The Cornice of mahogany, may come fo low as to hide the curtain-rods.

Plate 96. To this defign the Cornice will look well japanned. The curtain to this bed is drawn up and faftened by lines at the head, or with a loop and button.

Plate 97. This defign has a fweep top: the ornaments and cornice may be of mahogany, or gilt. To this bed is added a ftuffed head-board, with ornaments and drapery over it. The drapery may be the fame as the furniture or the lining: the ornaments gilt; the *head-board* is ftuffed, and projects like as the back of a fofa. The addition of ftuffed head-boards gives an elegant and high finifh to the appearance of beds. The curtains here are drawn up in double drapery, and faftened by lines at the head.

Plate 98. This defign has a Venetian or waggon top; the ornaments on which, with the cornice, may be japanned; the pending ornaments under the cornice are intended to act and ferve as a Vallance; may be either gilt or japanned. The bafes are enriched with feftooned drapery.

Plate 99. Defign for a Bed, with a low dome-top, and projecting front. The cornice and ornaments to this defign fhould be gilt. The arms to the head-board, if cut in low relief by a fkilful workman, and gilt, will have a lively effect.

Plate 100. To this defign a dome-top is given: the inner part

of

of which may be in the fame form ; the cornice and enrichments of gold burnifhed in parts.   The curtains to this bed are feftooned by lines which draw at the head.   This defign is proper for fatin or vel-vet furniture.

Plate 101.   Defign for a bed with a fquare dome-top.   The inner part in the fame manner.   The cornice will look well japanned or gilt.   The vallance to this bed is enriched with feftooned drapery. In this defign the effect of a ftuffed head-board and drapery are com-pletely fhewn.

Field Beds.   Two defigns are here given, which fhew the manner of hanging the furniture, and placing the ornaments.

Plate 104 fhews the various *fweeps* or *fhapes* in which Field Bed-tops may be made.

Prefs Beds.   Of thefe we have purpofely omitted to give any de-figns : their general appearance varying fo little from wardrobes, which piece of furniture they are intended to reprefent, that defigns for them were not neceffary.   The Wardrobe, Plate 85, has all the appearance of a Prefs-Bed ; in which cafe the upper drawers would be only fham, and form part of the door which may be made to turn up all in one piece, and form a tefter ; or may open in the middle, and fwing on each fide ; the under-drawer is ufeful to hold parts of the bed-furniture ; may be 5 feet 6 inches high, and 4 feet wide.

BED

BED PILLARS.

PLATES 105, 106, contain eight different defigns for Bed Pillars. The feet to three defigns; on Plate 106, are called Term Feet; and are intended to be fhewn when the bed is complete, as in Plate 100, &c.

CORNICES FOR BEDS OR WINDOWS.

NINE defigns for Cornices, which are fuitable for Beds or Windows, are here fhewn: thefe may be executed in wood painted and japanned, or in gold. A mixture of thefe two manners produces an elegant and grand effect. The foliage may be gilt, and the ground-work painted: or, the reverfe, the defigns marked **C F G** are intended to be all gilt—with parts matted and burnifhed.

CANDLE STANDS.

THESE are very ufeful in large fuits of apartments, as the light may be placed in any part at pleafure—in drawing-rooms, in halls and on large ftair-cafes, they are frequently ufed. Thefe defigns may be executed in mahogany or wood japanned. The branches to the defigns, Plate 110, fhould be of lacquered brafs.

LAMPS.

L A M P S.

FOUR defigns are here given, as neceffary to complete a fuit of furniture.   The ornaments are of brafs-work—the fquare one may be wrought in mahogany.

G I R A N D O L E S.

THIS kind of ornament admits of great variety in pattern and in elegance: they are ufually executed of the beft carved work—gilt and burnifhed in parts.   They may be carved, and coloured fuitable to the room.   The ftar in the defign, Plate 113, is intended to be of cut glafs, either white or coloured.

P I E R   G L A S S E S.

FOR Glaffes, a great variety of patterns may be invented.   The frames to Glaffes are almoft invariably of good carved work, gilt and burnifhed.   Six defigns for fquare glaffes are here fhewn, which is the fhape moft in fafhion at this time: they fhould be made nearly to fill the pier.   Plate 118 contains two defigns for Glaffes of the neweft fafhion, proper to be placed over Chimney Pieces, Sofas, &c. they muft be fixed very low.   The pannels of the fides are frequently made of various coloured glafs.

T E R M S   F O R   B U S T S

ARE generally made of mahogany, with the ornaments carved; their height muft be regulated by the fubject they are intended to support.

support.   The height, for a Bust as large as life, is between 3 and 4 feet.

CORNICES, BASE, *and* SUR-BASE MOULDINGS

for Library-Cases, Book-Cases, Wardrobes, &c. at large

PLATE 121 contains seven designs for *Cornices at large*, with a scale to shew the exact measurement of the several mouldings.   In general, Cornices for these purposes are wrought of all mahogany. We have known the ornaments in the frieze, inlaid with various coloured woods, or painted, produce a good effect.   Plate 122 contains four more designs for *Cornices*, and six Designs for *Base Mouldings*. Plate 123 contains eleven designs for *Sur-base Mouldings*.

Having gone through a complete series or suit of Household Furniture, we were strongly advised to draw out a plan, which should shew the manner of properly disposing of the same : with this intent, aided by the advice of some experienced friends, we here shew, at one view, the necessary and proper furniture for a *Drawing-room*, and also for a *Dining-room* or *Parlour*, subject to the following variations :

If the object of this plan was a *Drawing-room* only—on each side the chimney-piece there should be a sofa, and on the opposite side, instead of a sofa, should be a confidante: the side-board also should be removed, and an elegant commode substituted in the place ; the remaining space may be filled up with chairs.

For a *Dining-room*, instead of the Pier-tables, should be a set of dining-tables : the rest of the furniture, and the general ordonnance of

the

the room is equally proper, except the glaſs over the ſofa, which might be omitted : but this is mere opinion, many of the **Dining Parlours** of our firſt nobility having full as much glaſs as is here ſhewn.

The proper furniture for a Drawing-room, and for a Dining-room or Parlour, being thus pointed out, it remains only to obſerve, that the general appearance of the latter ſhould be plain and neat, while the former, being conſidered as a State-room, ſhould poſſeſs all the elegance embelliſhments can give.

F I N I S.

THE

CABINET-MAKER

AND

UPHOLSTERER's GUIDE, &c.

Pl. 1.

Chairs.

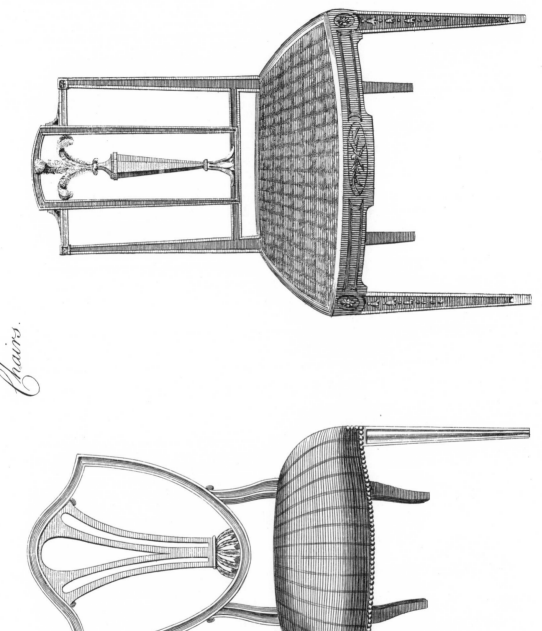

London. Published Sept.r 1.st 1787. by I & J. Taylor. N.o 56. High Holborn.

Pl. 2

d

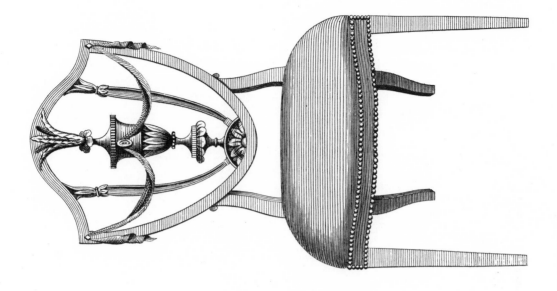

Chairs.

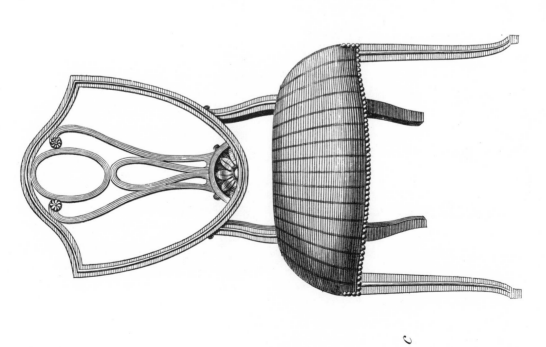

c

London Published Sept.r 1.st 1787, by I. & J. Taylor. N.o 56 High Holborn.

Pl. 3

Chairs.

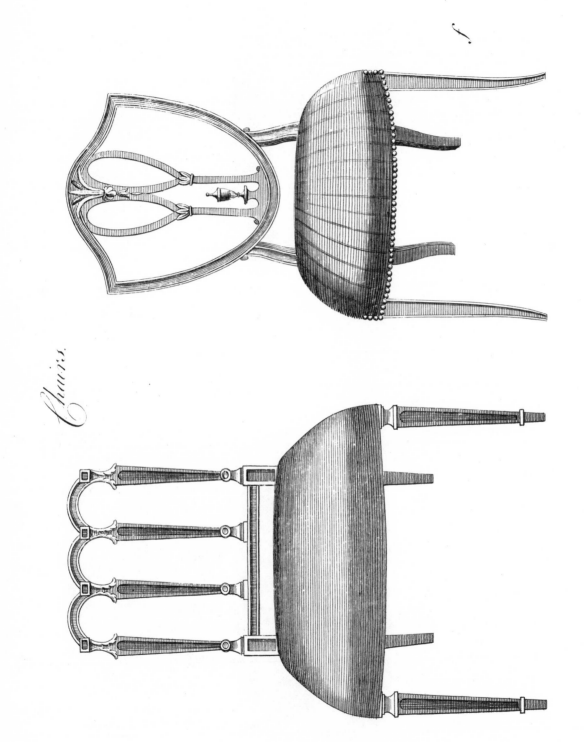

London, Published Sept.ᵉ 1.ˢᵗ 1787, by I.& I.Taylor, N.º 56. High Holborn.

Pl. 4

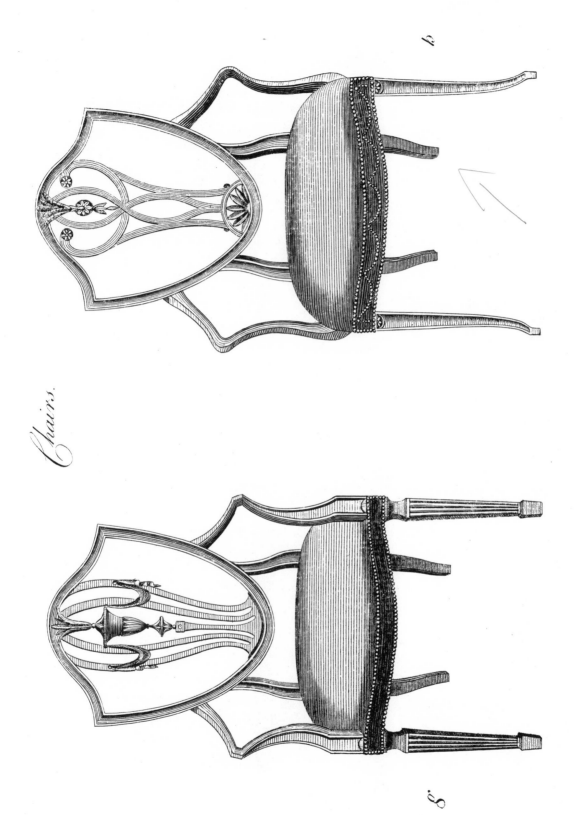

Chairs.

London, Published Sept.1.st 1787. by I.& J. Taylor, N.o 56 High Holborn.

Pl. 5

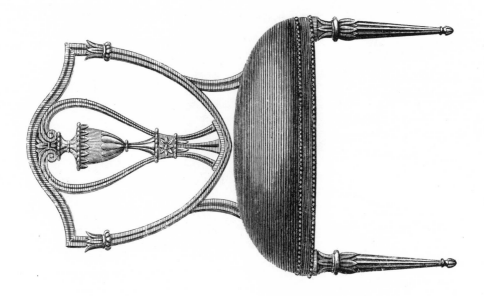

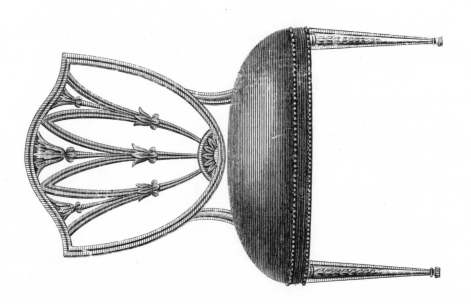

London. Published by I.&J. Taylor, N°.56. Holborn.

Pl. 6

Chairs.

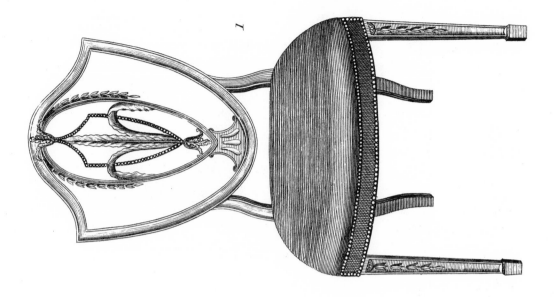

1

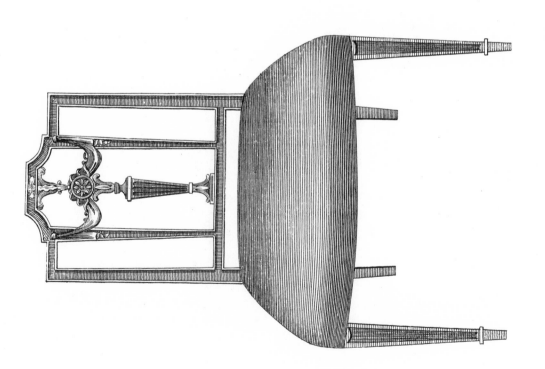

London, Published by I. & J. Taylor, No. 56. High Holborn, July 2, 1787.

Pl. 7

Chairs.

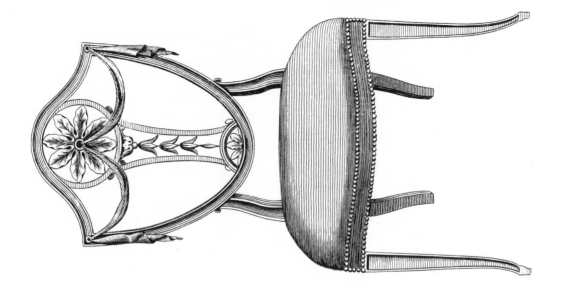

Q

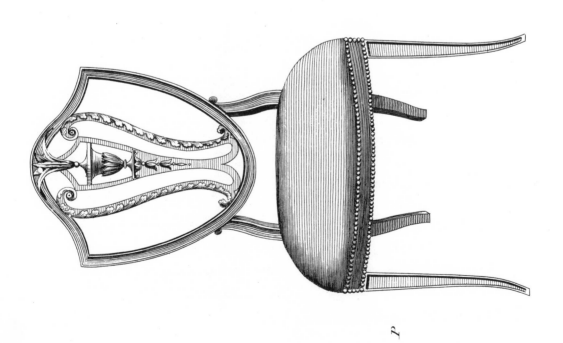

P

London. Published Sept.r 1.st 1787. by I. & J. Taylor, N.o 56, High Holborn.

Pl. 8

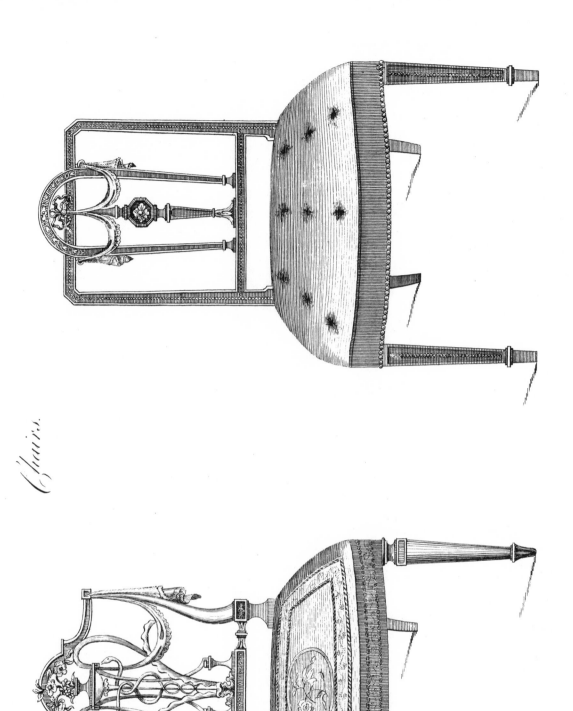

Chairs.

London, Published Sept.r 1.st 1787. by I.&J.Taylor, N.o 56. High Holborn.

Pl. 9

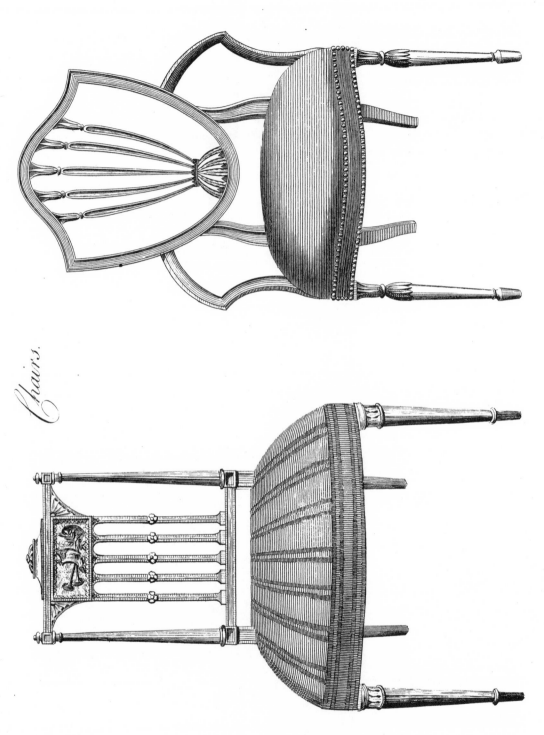

Chairs.

Z

Y

London Published Sept. 1.st 1787, by I. & I. Taylor. N.º 56. High Holborn.

Pl.9

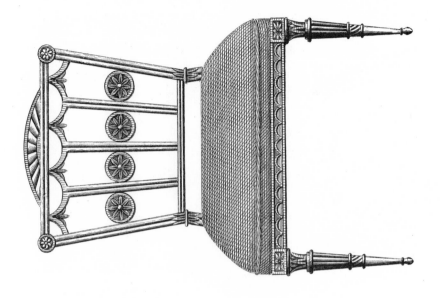

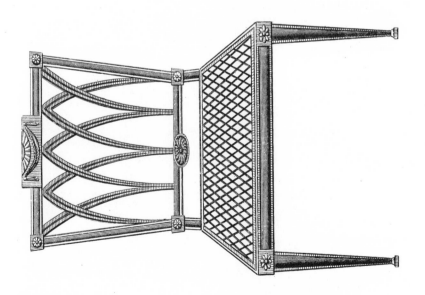

London, Published by I. & J. Taylor, N.º 56, Holborn.

Pl. 10

Cabriole Chairs.

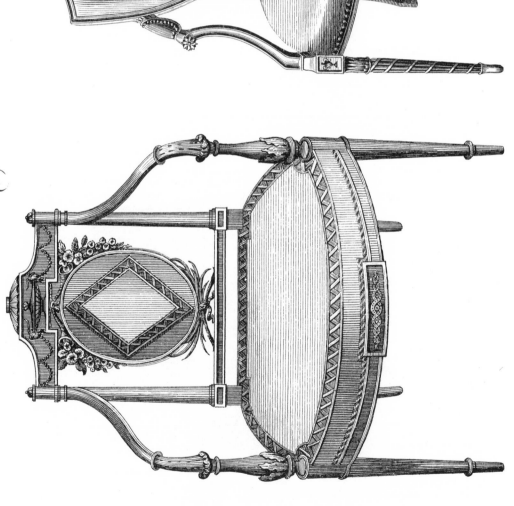

London, Published by I.&J. Taylor, N°. 56, High Holborn, July 2, 1787.

Cabriole Chairs.

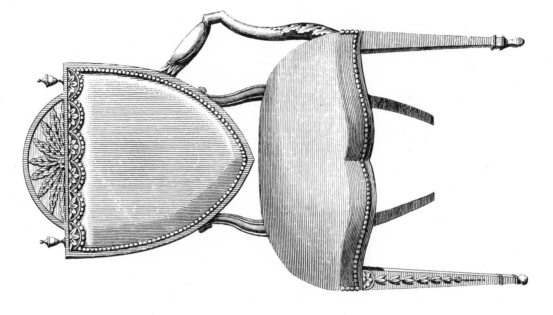

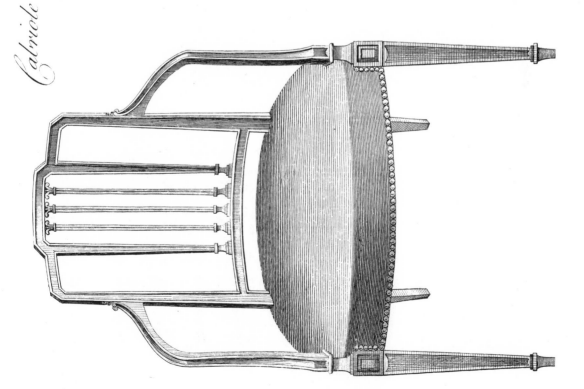

London, Published Oct.r 2.nd 1787. by I.& J. Taylor, No.56. High Holborn.

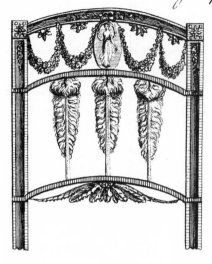

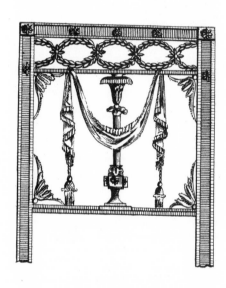

London, Published Jan.1.1794. by I.& J.Taylor, Holborn.

London, Published Jan.1.1794, by I. & J.Taylor, Holborn.

Pl. 14

Hall Chairs.

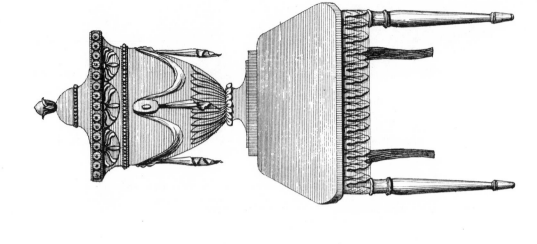

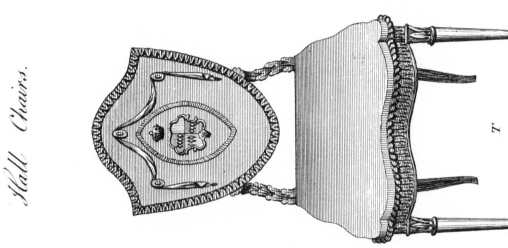

T

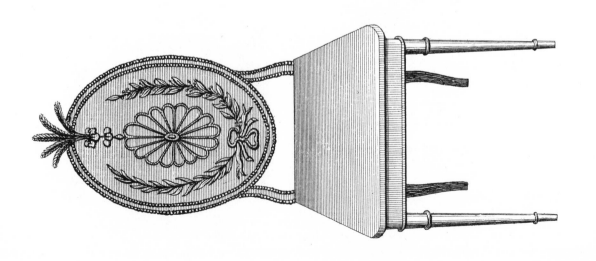

London, Published Sept.r 1.st 1787, by I. & J. Taylor, N.o 56 High Holborn.

Pl. 45.

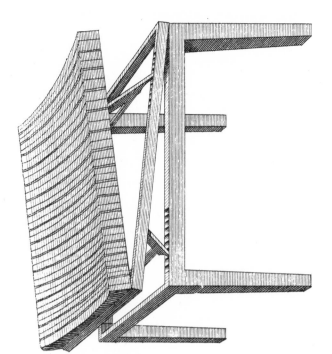

Gouty Stool.

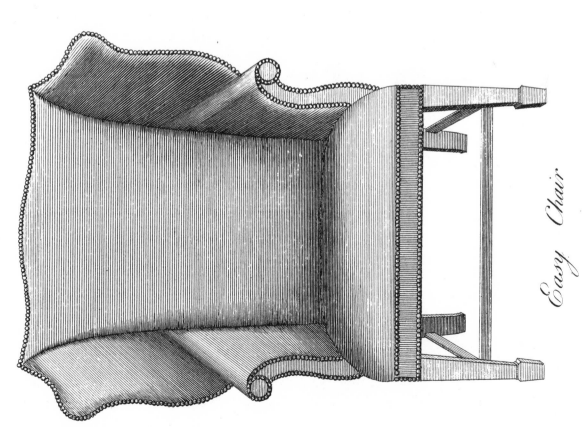

Easy Chair.

London. Published Octr. 1st 1787, by I.&.J. Taylor. N° 56. High Holborn.

Pl. 16

Stools.

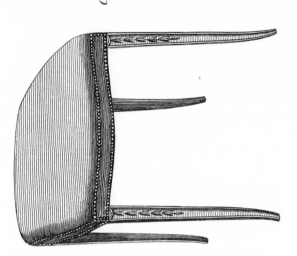

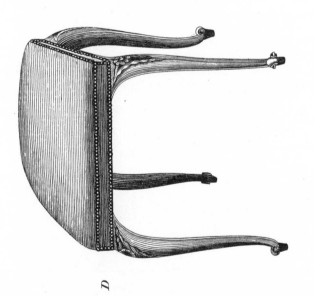

London, Published by I.&I.Taylor. N.º 56, High Holborn, July 2.ª 1787.

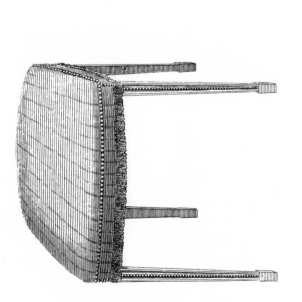

Pl. 17

Stools.

O

N

London, Published Sept.r 1.st 1787, by I.& J. Taylor, N.o 56 High Holborn.

Pl. 18

Window Stools.

A

B

London, Published by I. & J. Taylor, N.º 56, High Holborn, July 2, 1787.

Pl. 19

i

Window Stools.

k

London, Published Sept.r 1st 1787, by I. & J. Taylor, No. 56, High Holborn.

Pl. 22

D

Sofa.

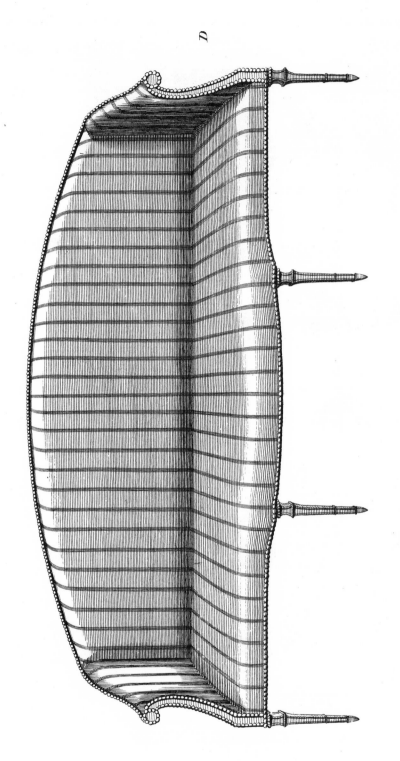

London, Published Sept.r 1.st 1787, by I. & J. Taylor, N.o 56. High Holborn.

Pl. 23

Sofa.

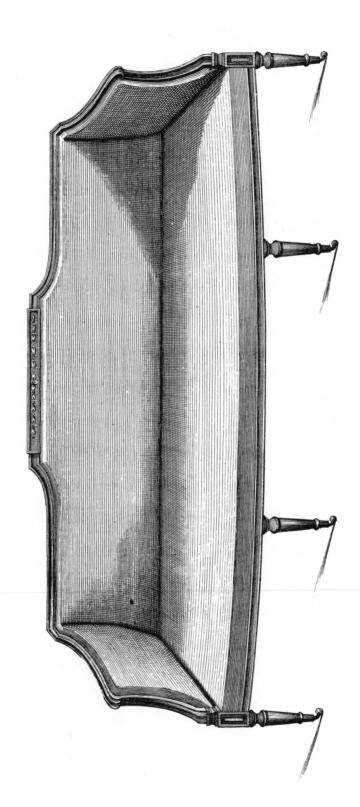

London, Published Oct.r 2.d, 1787, by I.& J. Taylor, N.o 56, High Holborn.

Pl. 24

Sofa.

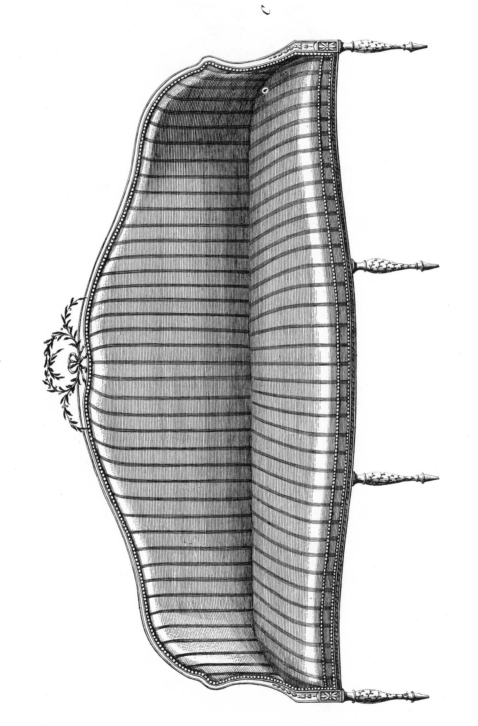

London, Published Sept.r 1.st 1787, by I.&J.Taylor, No.56.High Holborn.

Pl. 25

Sofa.

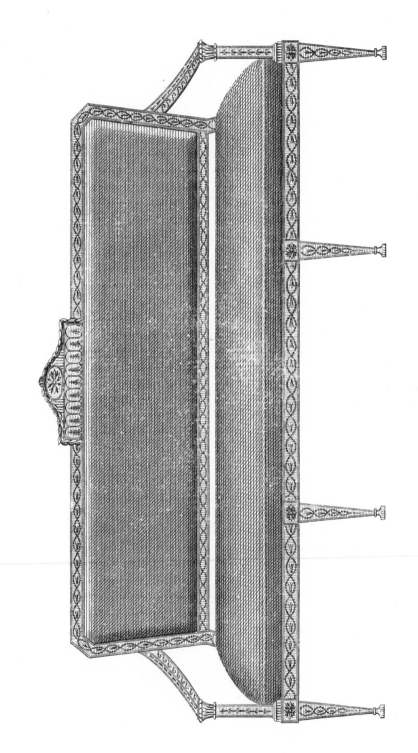

London. Printed for I.& J.Taylor, N.°56. Holborn.

Pl. 26

Bar back Sofa.

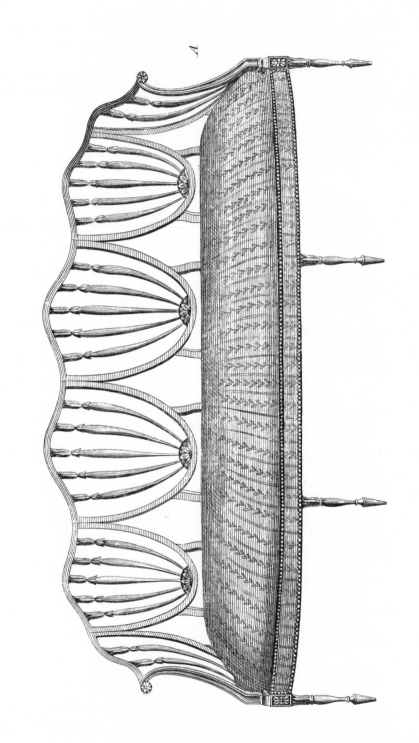

A

London, Published by I. & J. Taylor, N.º 56. High Holborn, July 2, 1787.

Pl. 27

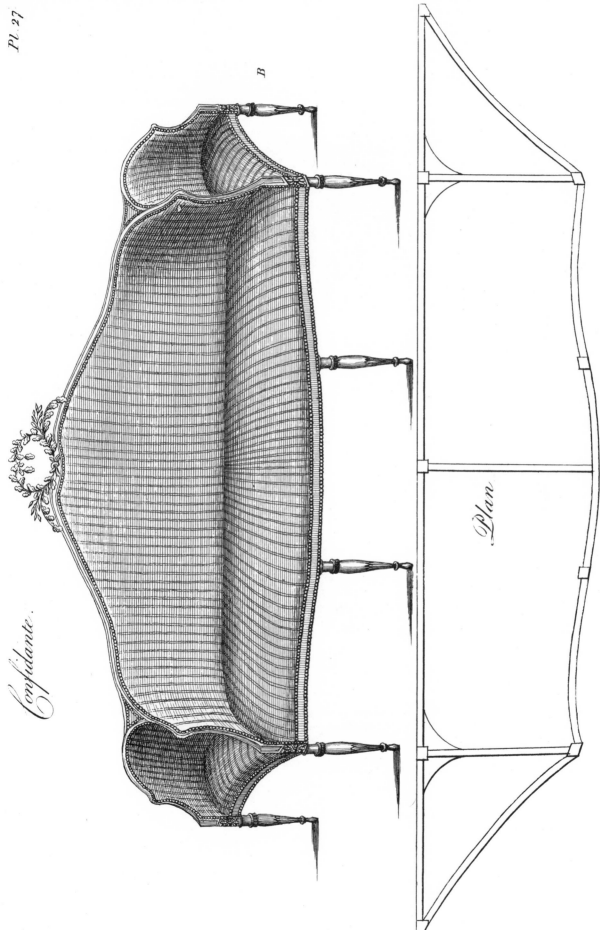

Confidante.

B

Plan

London, Published by I.&J. Taylor, N° 56, High Holborn, July 2, 1787.

Pl. 28

Duchefse.

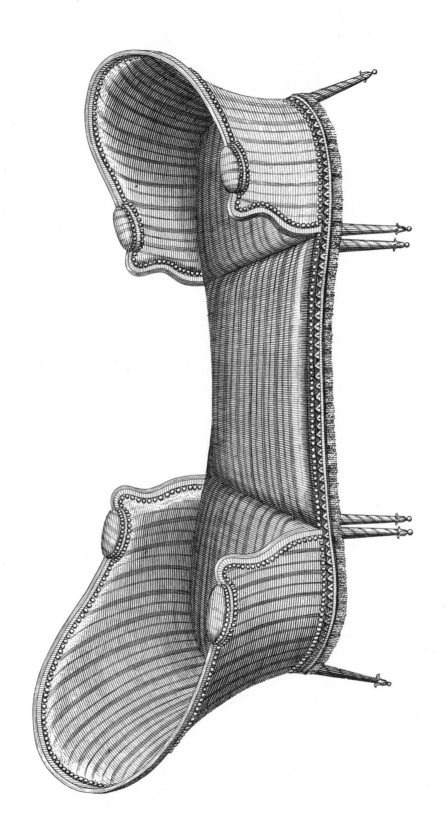

London, Published Oct.r 1.st 1787, by I. & J. Taylor, N.o 56. High Holborn.

Pl. 29

Side Board.

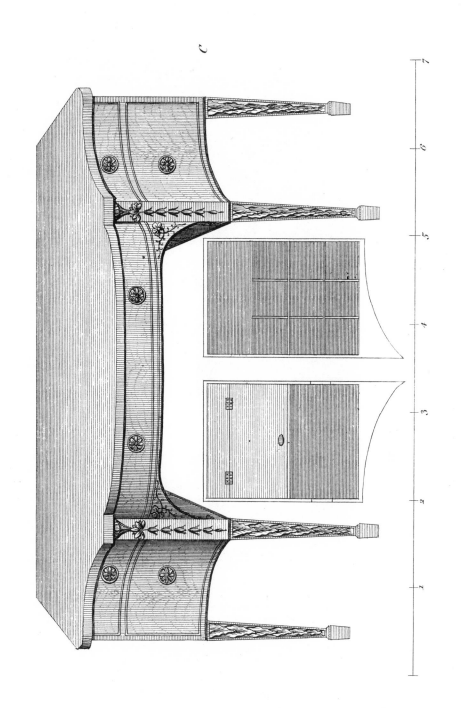

c

London, Published Sept.r 1.st 1787, by I.&J.Taylor, N.o 56, High H.born.

Pl. 30

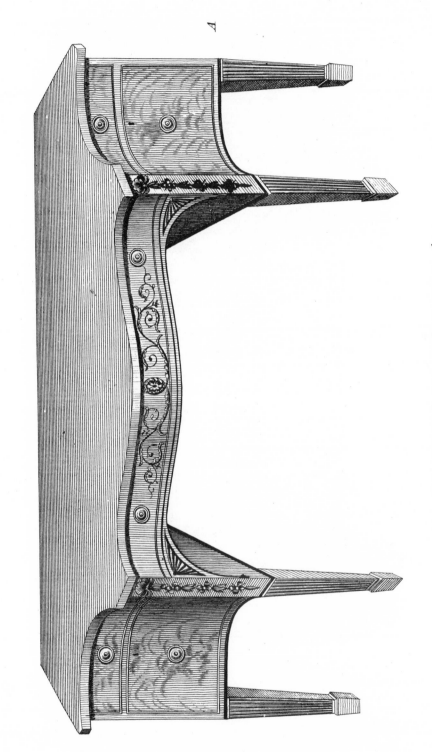

Side Board.

A

London, Published by I. & J. Taylor, N.º 56. High Holborn, July 2.1787.

Pl. 31

Side Board.

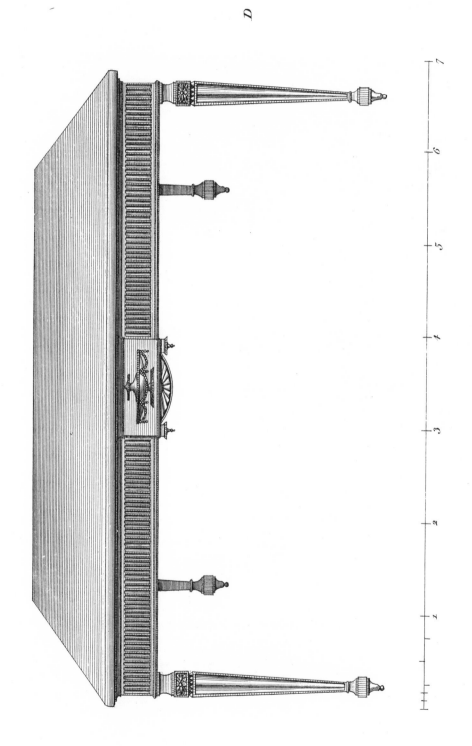

D

London, Published Sept.r 1.st 1787, by I.&J.Taylor,N.o 56. High Holborn.

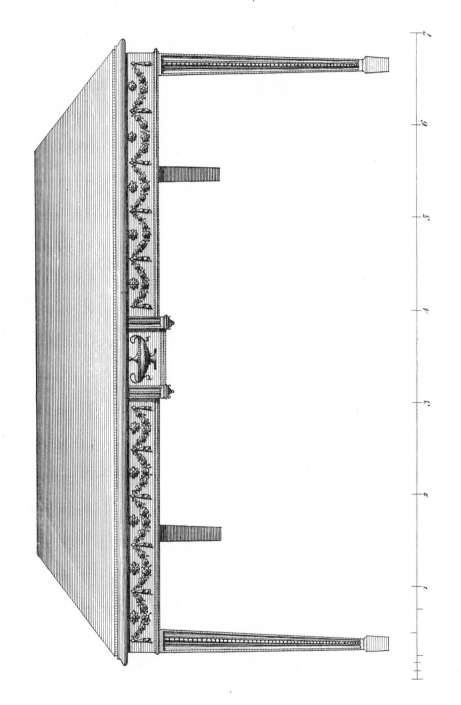

Pl. 32

Side Board.

E

London, Published Sept.r 1.st 1787, by I. & J. Taylor, N.o 56, High Holborn.

Pl. 33

Side Board.

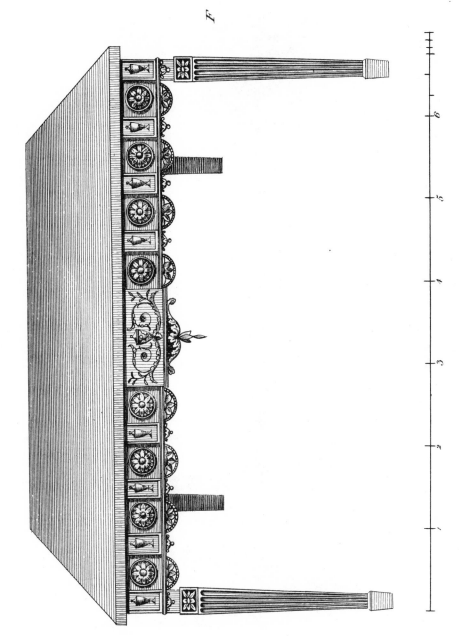

F

London Published Sept.¹ 1.ˢᵗ 1787. by I. & J. Taylor, N.º 56. High Holborn.

Pl. 34

Side Board.

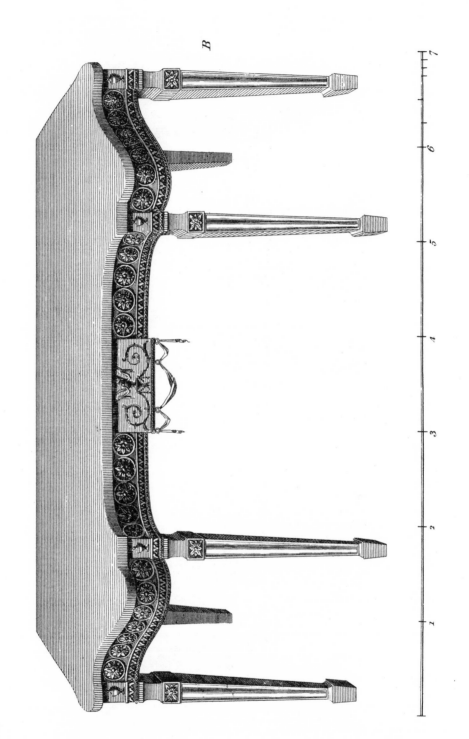

B

1   2   3   4   5   6   7

London, Published by I.& J. Taylor, N.º 56. High Holborn, July 2.ª 1787.

Pl. 35

Pedestals and Vases.

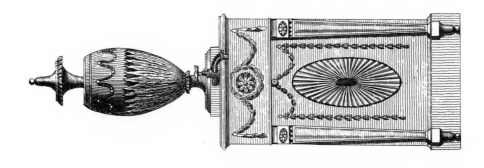

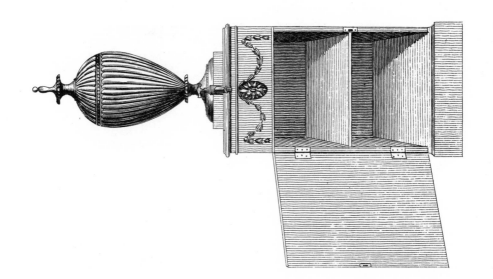

London. Published by I. & J. Taylor, Nº 56. High Holborn, July 2,1787.

Pl. 36

Pedestals and Vases.

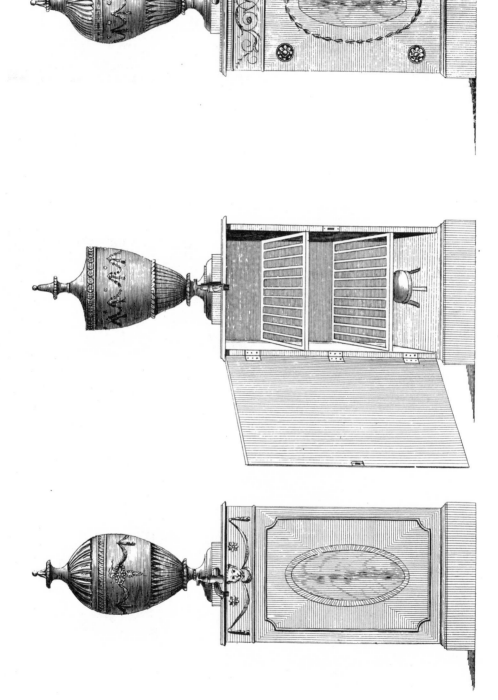

London, Published July 2, 1787, by I. & J. Taylor, N°.56. High Holborn.

Pl. 37

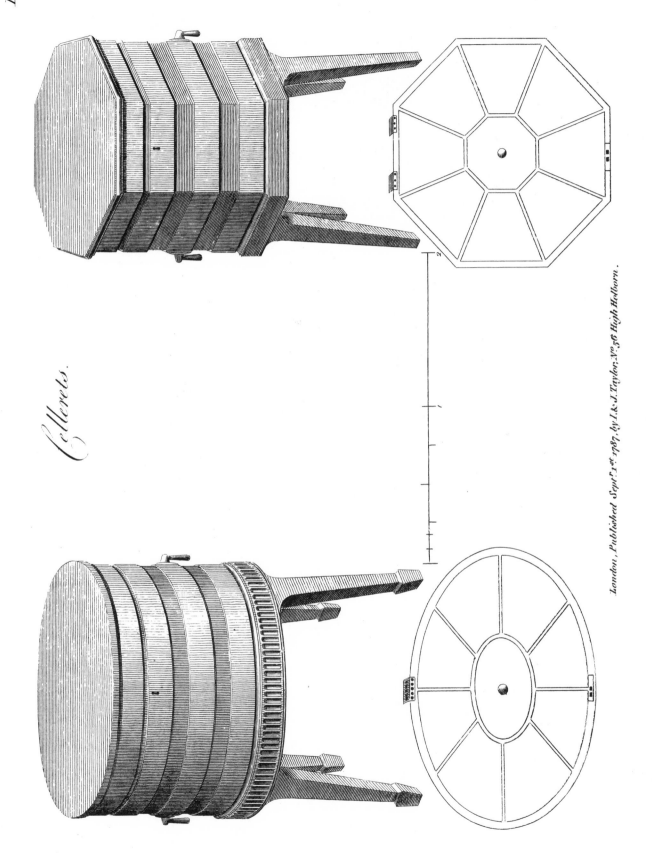

Cellerets.

London, Published Sept.r 1.st 1787, by I & J. Taylor, No. 56 High Holborn.

Pl.38

Knife Cases.

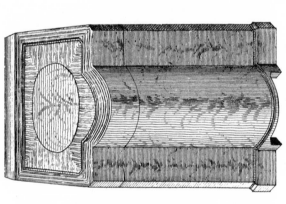

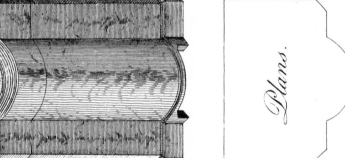

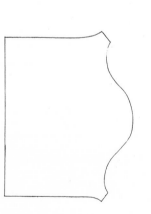

Plans.

London. Published by I.& J. Taylor. N.º 56. High Holborn. Sep.ᵗ 1.ˢᵗ 1787.

Pl. 39

Knife Cases.

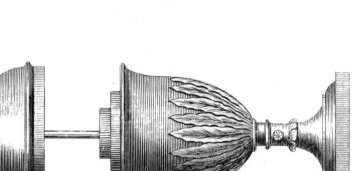
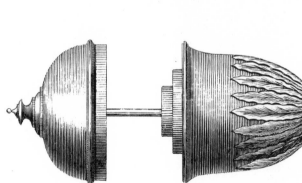
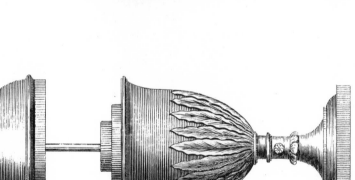
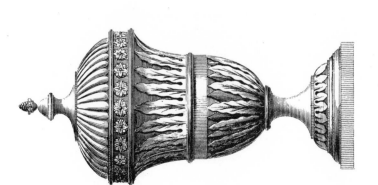

London, Published by I.& J. Taylor, N.° 56, High Holborn, July 2.1787.

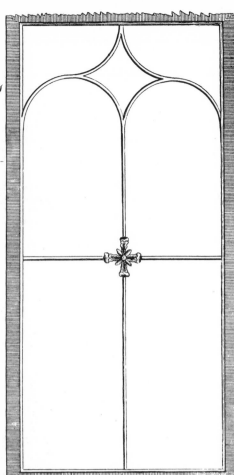

Doors for Book-Cases, &c.

Pl. 40

Desk and Bookcase.

C

London, Published by I&J Taylor, Nº 56, High Holborn. July 1. 1787.

Pl. 41

Desk and Bookcase.

D

London, Published by I.& J. Taylor, N.º 56, High Holborn, July 2,1787.

Pl. 42

Desk and Bookcase.

E

1 2 3 4 5

London, Published July 2, 1787, by I.& J. Taylor, N.°. 56, High Holborn.

Pl. 43

Secretary and Bookcase.

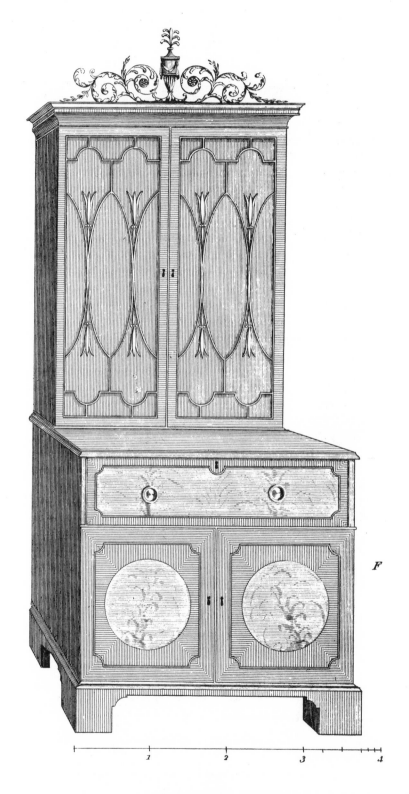

F

London, Published July 2, 1787, by I. & J. Taylor, Nº 56, High Holborn.

Pl. 44

Secretary and Bookcase.

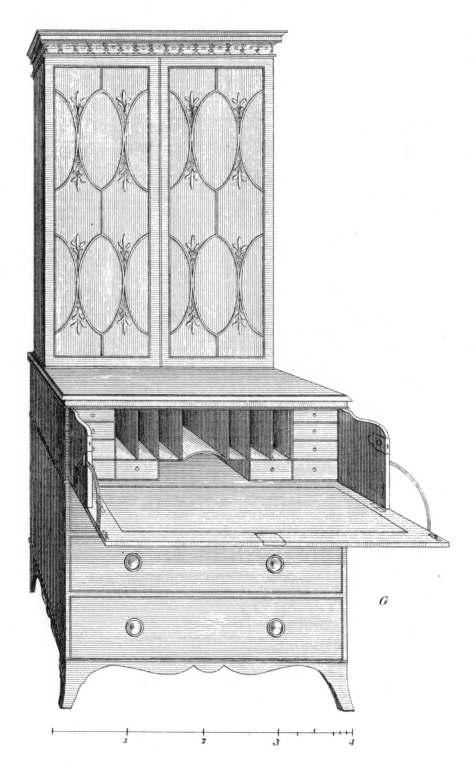

G

London, Published July 2, 1787, by I.& J. Taylor N°. 56, High Holborn.

Pl. 45

End View.

Library Case.

A

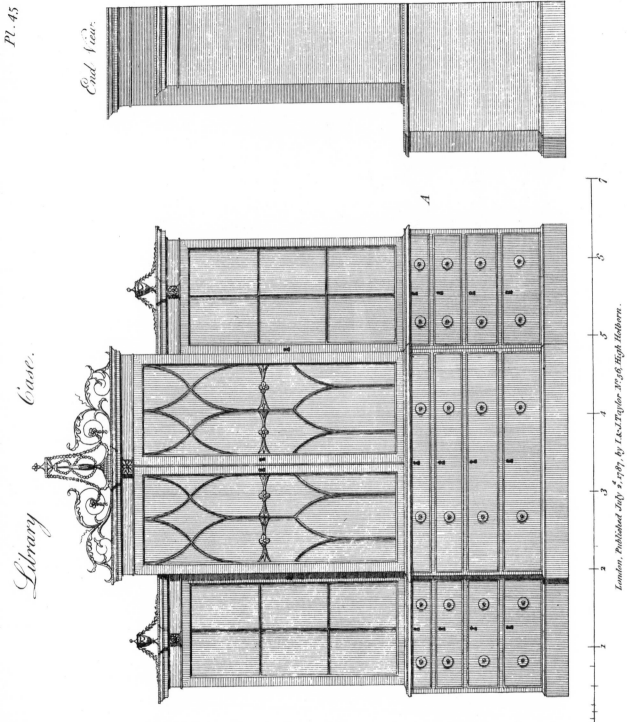

London, Published July 2, 1787, by I.& J.Taylor N°.56, High Holborn.

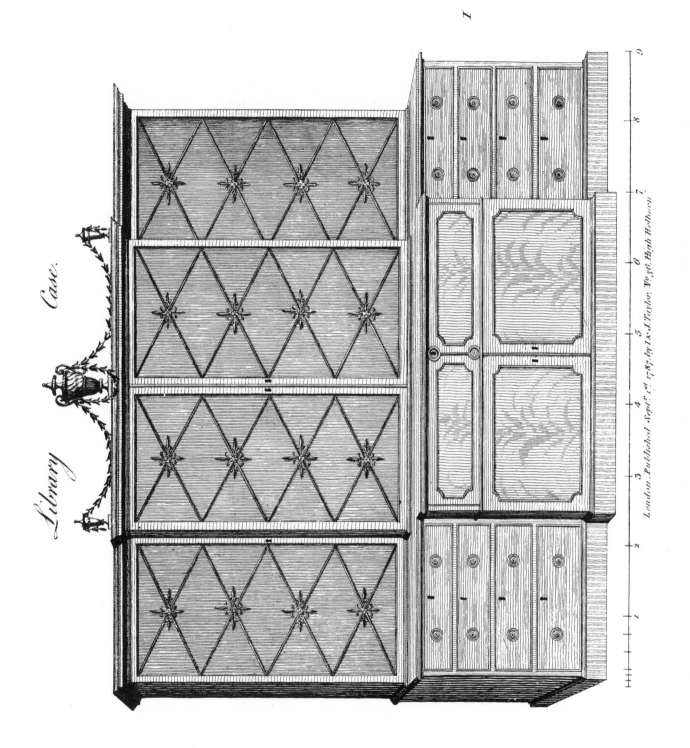

Pl. 46

Library Case.

London Published Sept.r 1.st 1787 by I.&.J.Taylor. N.o 56. High Holborn.

Pl. 47

Library Case.

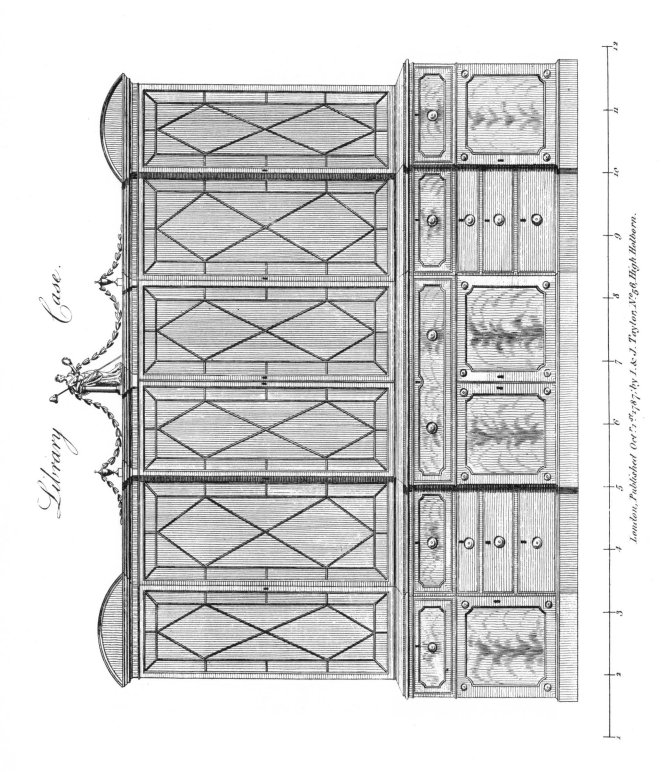

London, Published Oct.r 3.d 1787, by I.& J. Taylor, N.o 56, High Holborn.

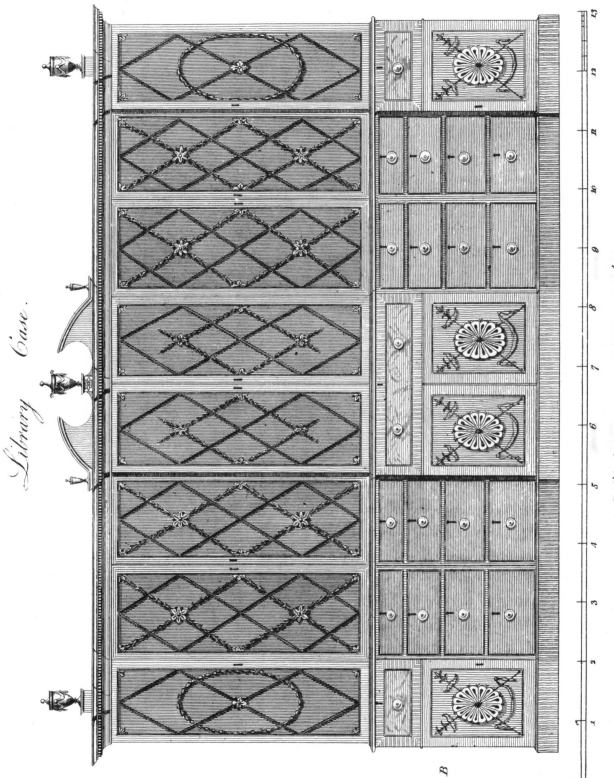

Pl. 48.

Library Case.

B

London, Published by I.& J.Taylor, N.° 56, High Holborn, July 2, 1787.

Pl. 49

Library Table.

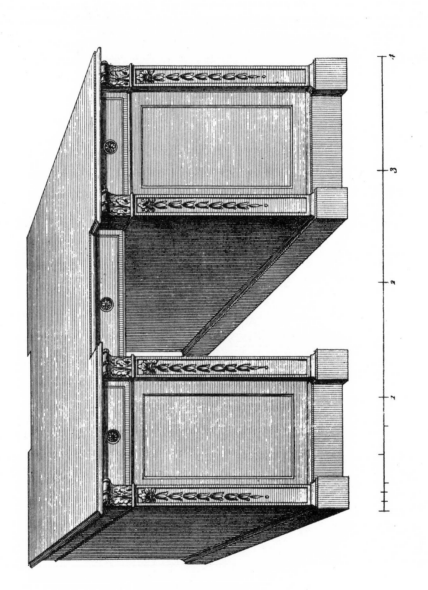

London, Published Sept.r 1.st 1787, by I.& J.Taylor, N.o 5 & 6. High Holborn.

Pl. 50

Library Tables.

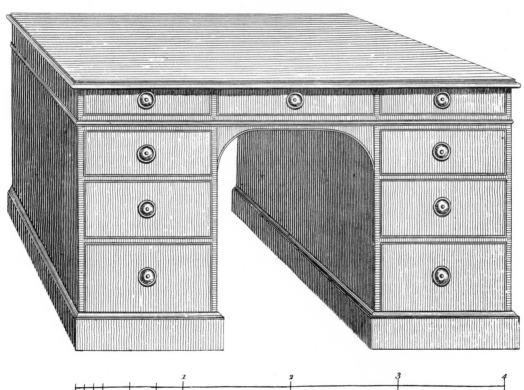

London, Published Oct.r 1.st 1787, by I. & J. Taylor, N.o 56, High Holborn.

Pl. 51

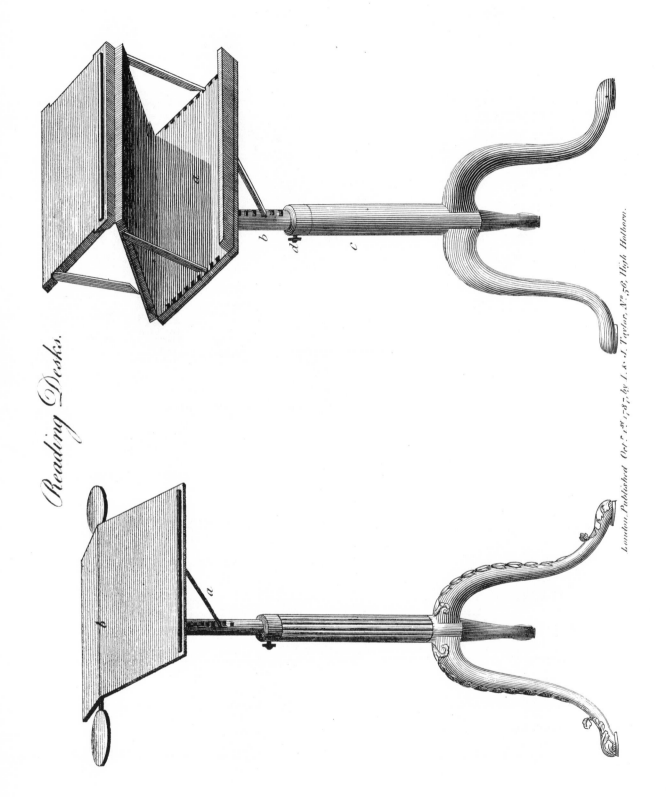

Reading Desks.

London. Published Oct.ʳ 1.ᵗᵉ 1787, by I. & J. Taylor, No. 56, High Holborn.

B

C

London, Published July 2.ᵈ, 1787, by I.& J. Taylor N.º 56, High Holborn.

Pl. 53

Double Chest of Drawers.

A

London, Published by I. & J. Taylor, No 56, High Holborn, July 2, 1787.

Pl. 54

Double Chest of Drawers.

Plan

1   2   3   4

London, Published Sept.ʳ 1.ˢᵗ 1787, by I. & J. Taylor, N.º 56, High Holborn.

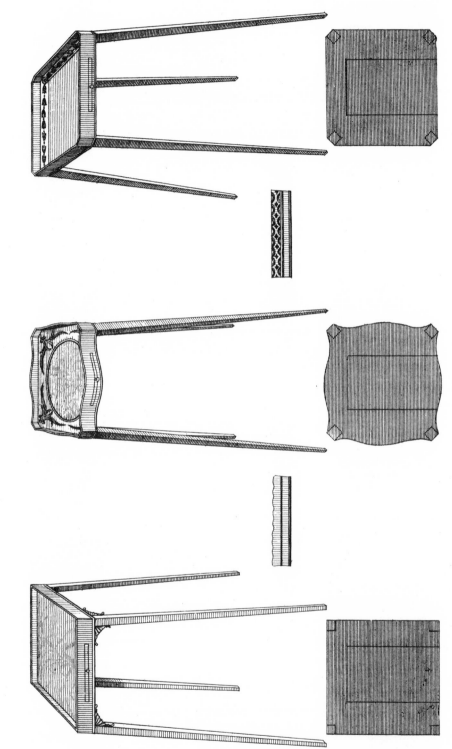

Pl. 55.

Urn Stands.

London, Published July 2ᵈ 1787, by I. & J. Taylor, Nᵒ 56, High Holborn.

Pl.56

Urn Stands.

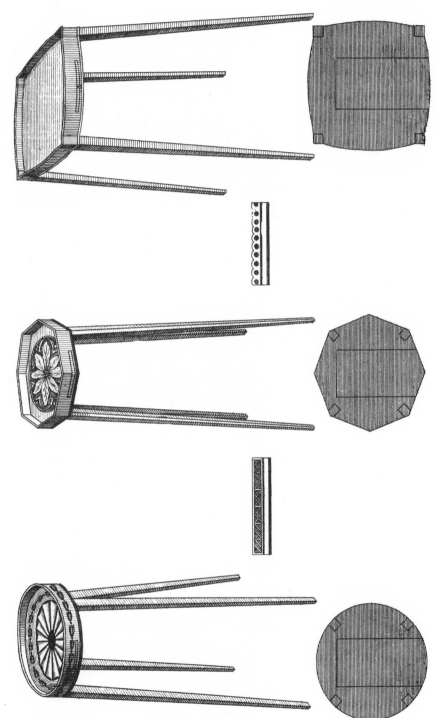

London, Published July 2 1787, by I. & I.Taylor, N°.56. High Holborn.

Pl. 57

Tea Caddies.

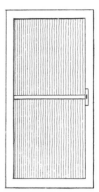

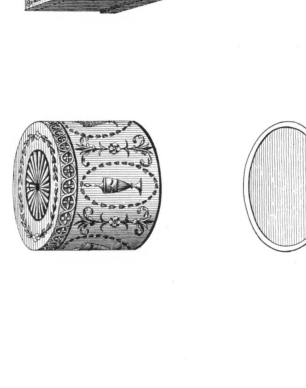

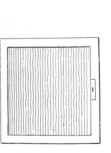

Plans.

London, Published Sept.ʳ 1.ˢᵗ 1787, by I.& J. Taylor, Nᵒ 56. High Holborn.

Pl. 58

Tea Chests.

Plans

London, Published Sept.r 1.st 1787, by I. & J. Taylor, N.o 56, High Holborn.

Pl.59

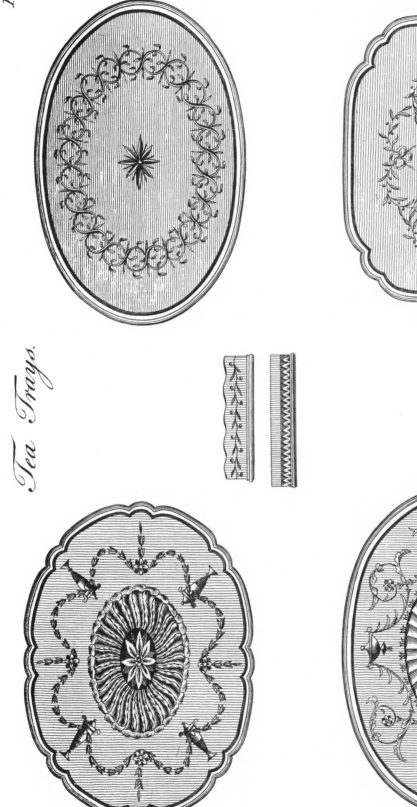

Tea Trays.

London, Published Oct.r 1.st 1787, by I.& J.Taylor, N.o 56.High Holborn.

Pl. 60

Card Tables.

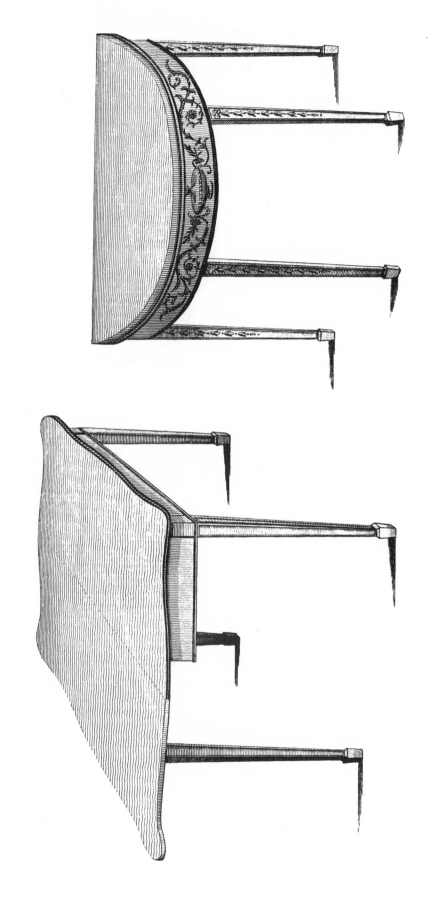

London. Published Sept.r 1.st 1787. by Ias. J. Taylor, N.o 56, High Holborn.

Pl. 61.

Tops for   *Card Tables.*

London, Published Oct.r 1.st 1787, by I.& J. Taylor, N.o 56, High Holborn.

Pl. 62

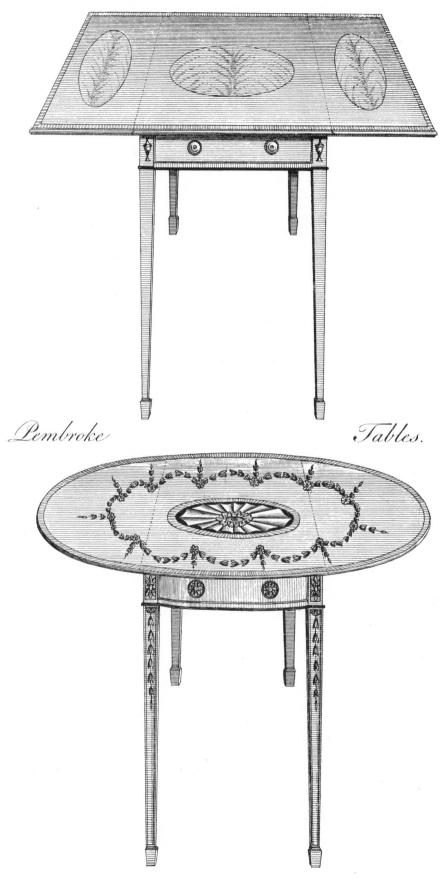

Pembroke   *Tables.*

London, Published Sept.r 1.st 1787, by I.& J.Taylor, N.o 56, High Holborn.

Pl. 63

Tops for Pembroke Tables, &c.

London, Published Septr 1.st 1787, by I. & J. Taylor, N.º 56, High Holborn.

Pl. 64

Pier Tables.

C

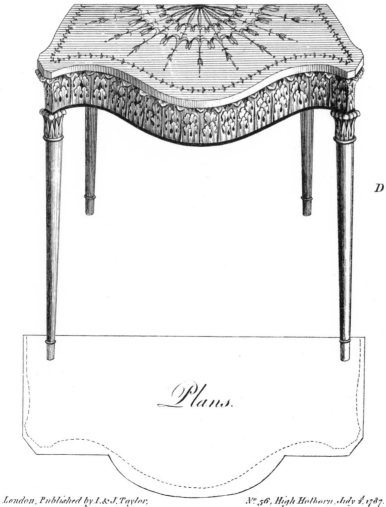

Plans.

D

London, Published by I. & J. Taylor. Nᵒ. 56, High Holborn, July 1ˢᵗ. 1787.

Pl. 65

A

Pier Tables.

B

London, Published by I.& J.Taylor, N⁰ 56,High Holborn, July 2.1787.

Pl.66

Tops for   *Pier Tables, &c.*

London, Published July 2, 1787, by I. & J. Taylor, No. 56, High Holborn.

Pl. 67

Tambour Writing Table.

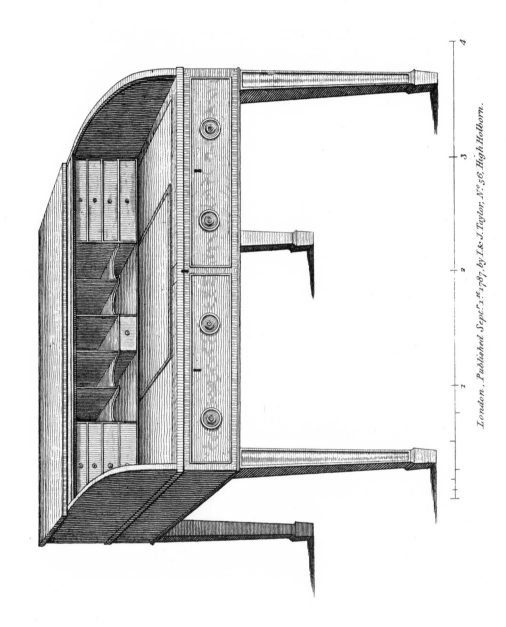

London, Published Sept.r 1.st 1787, by I.& J.Taylor, N.o 56. High Holborn.

Pl. 68.

Tambour Table.

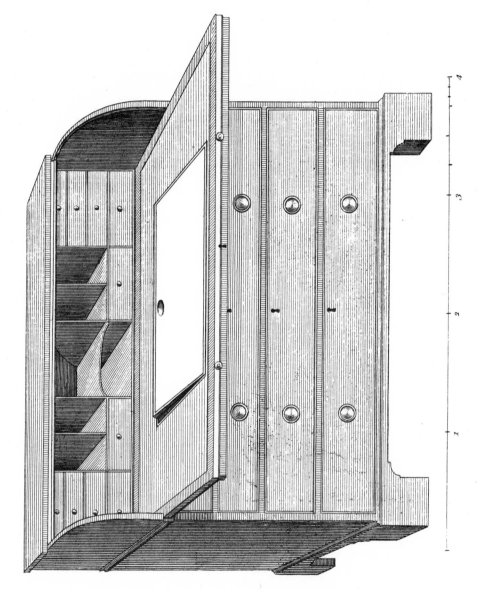

London. Published July 2, 1787, by I.&J. Taylor, Nᵒ 56, High Holborn.

Pl.69

Tambour Writing Table and Bookcase.

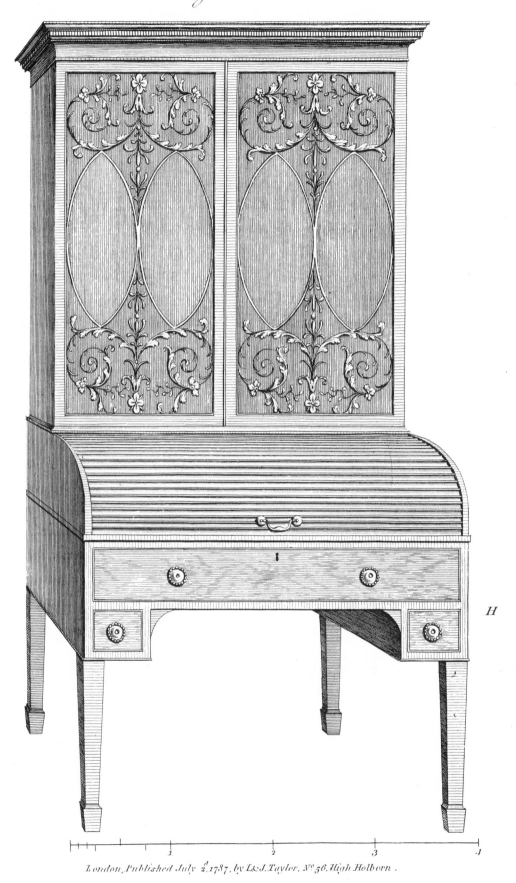

H

London, Published July 2.d 1787, by I.&J.Taylor, N.o 56, High Holborn.

Pl. 70

Dressing Glasses.

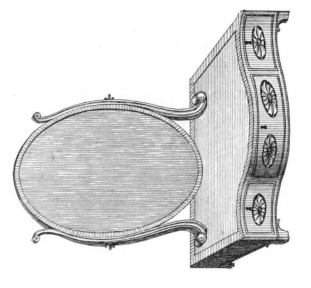

London, Published Sept.r 1.st 1787, by I.& J. Taylor, N.o 56, High Holborn.

Pl. 71

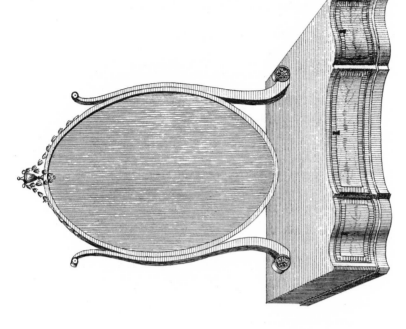

Dressing Glasses.

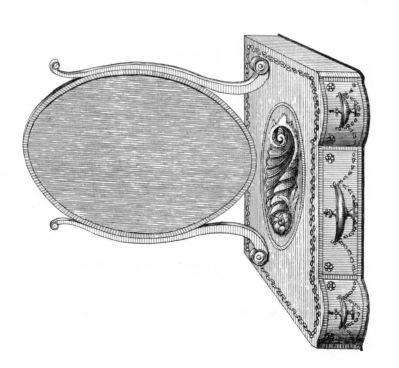

London, Published Septr 1.st 1787, by I. & J. Taylor, N.º 56, High Holborn.

Pl. 72

Ladies Dressing Tables.

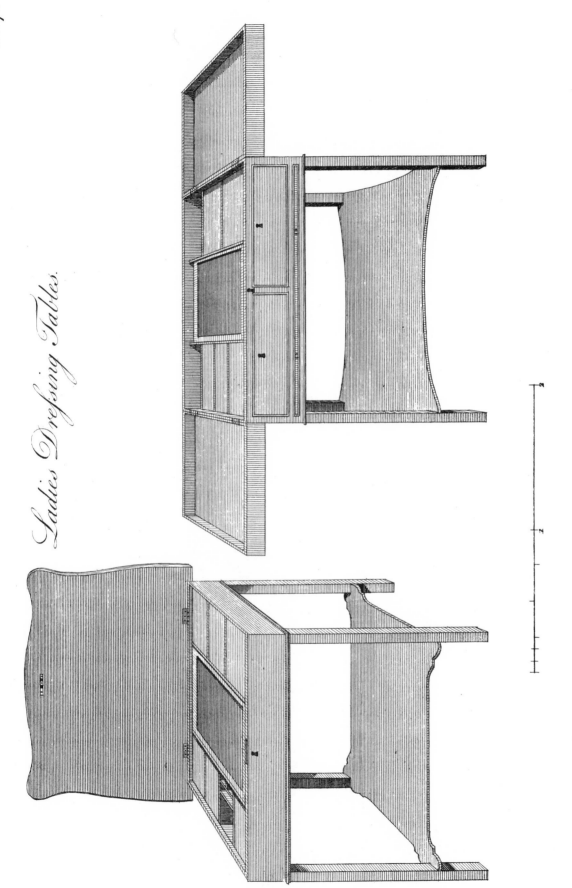

London, Published Oct.r 2.st 1787, by I.& J.Taylor, N.o 56. High Holborn.

Pl. 73

Ladies Dressing Tables.

London, Published Sep.t 1.st 1787, by I. & J. Taylor, N.o 56, High Holborn.

Pl. 74

Dressing Drawers.

London, Published Oct.r 1.st 1787, by I. & J. Taylor, N.o 56, High Holborn.

Pl. 75

Dressing Drawers.

London, Published Oct.ʳ 1ˢᵗ 1787, by I. & J. Taylor, Nº 56, High Holborn.

B

C

London, Published Sept.r 1.st 1787. by I. & J. Taylor, N.o 56. High Holborn.

Pl. 77

Commode Dreſsing Table.

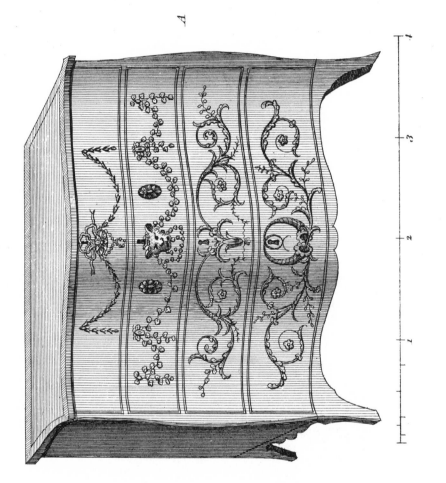

A

London, Published July 2ᵈ, 1787, by I. & J. Taylor, Nº.56, High Holborn.

Pl. 78

A Commode.

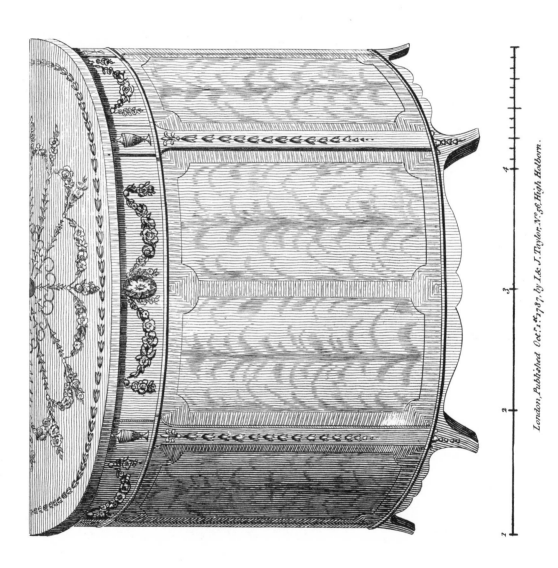

London, Published Oct.r 1.st 1787. by I. & J. Taylor, N.o 56. High Holborn.

Pl. 78 ✱

Tops for Dressing Tables,

and Commodes.

London, Published Oct.ʳ 1.ˢᵗ 1787, by I. & J. Taylor, Nº 56, High Holborn.

Pl. 79

Rudd's Table.

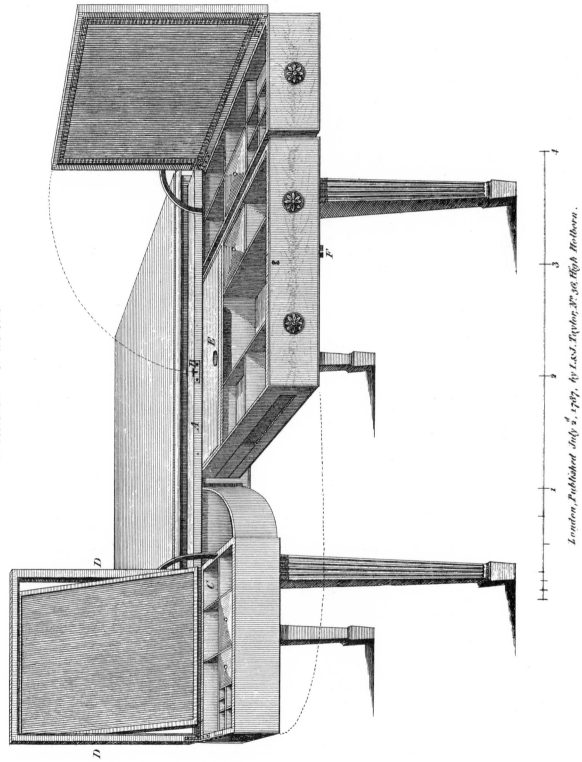

London, Published July 2, 1787, by I.&J. Taylor, No. 56, High Holborn.

Pl. 80

Shaving Tables.

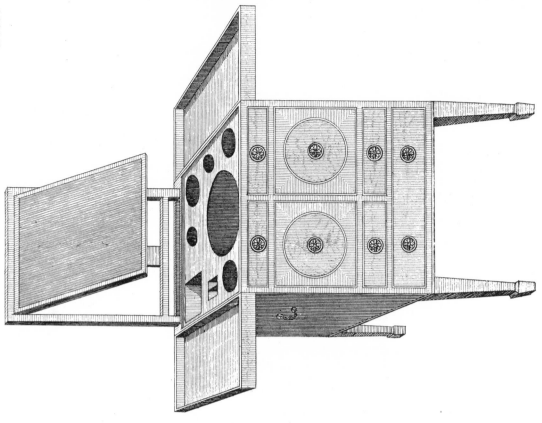

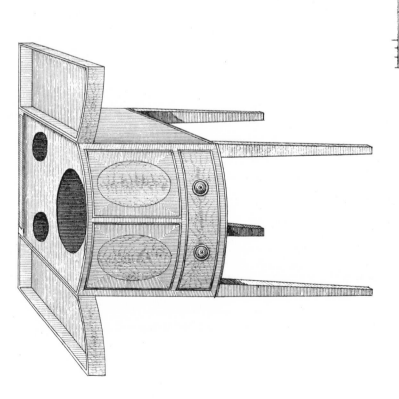

London, Published July 2, 1787, by I. & J. Taylor, N.º 56, High Holborn.

Pl. 81

Night Table.

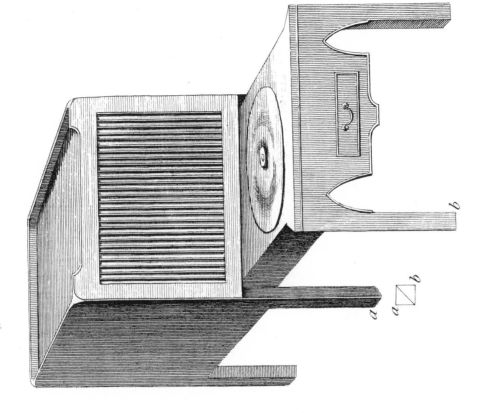

a

a □ *b*

b

Bidet   *Shaving*   *Table.*

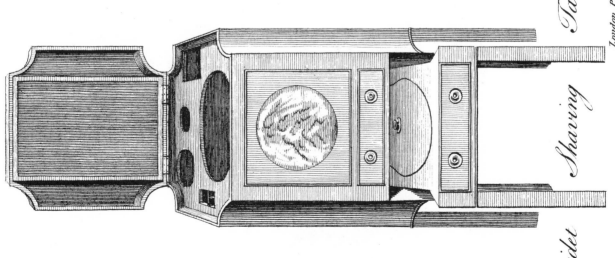

London, Published Oct'.1.st 1787, by I.&.J. Taylor, N°.56, High Holborn.

Pl. 82

Night Tables.

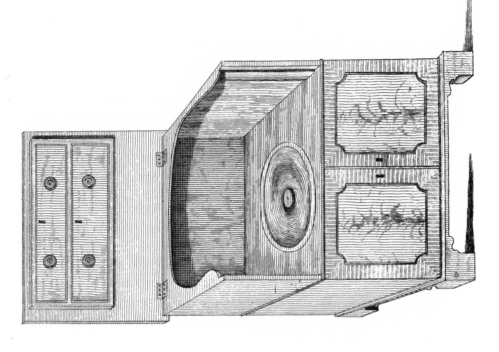

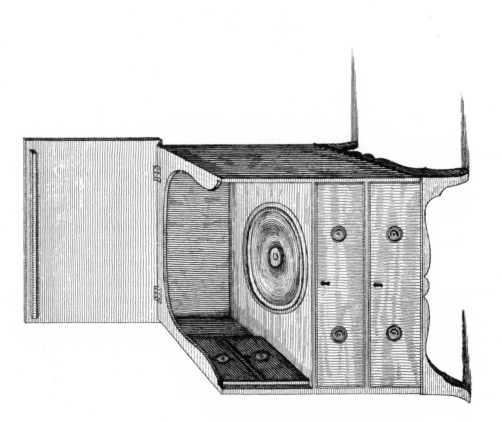

London, Published July 2, 1787, by I.&J.Taylor, N.º 56. High Holborn.

Pl. 83

Bidet.

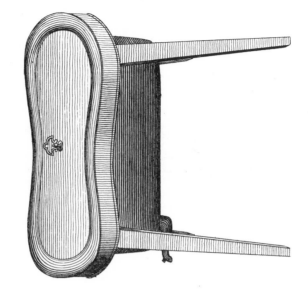

Bason Stand.

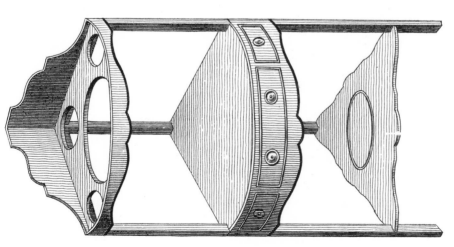

London, Published Oct.r 1.st 1787. by I.& J.Taylor, N.o 56.High Holborn.

Pl. 84

Bason Stands.

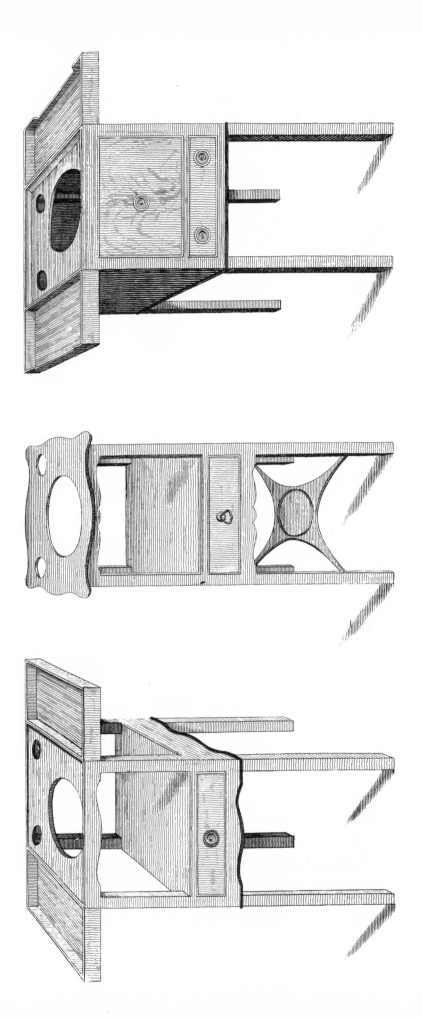

London, Published Sept.r 1.st 1787, by I.& J.Taylor, N.o 56. High Holborn.

Pl. 85

Wardrobe.

A

London, Published Sept.r 1st 1787, by I. & J. Taylor, No. 56, High Holborn.

Pl. 86

Wardrobe.

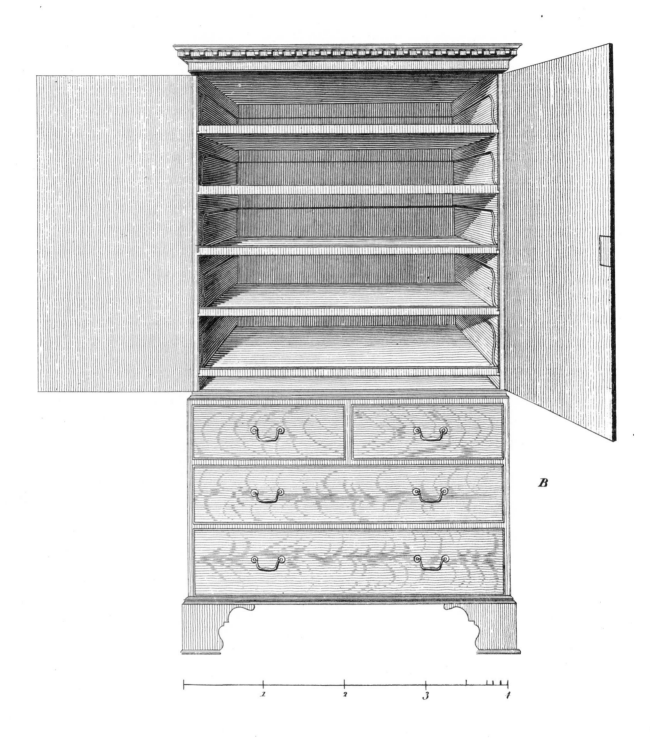

B

London, Published Sept.r 1st 1787, by I.& J. Taylor, No. 56, High Holborn.

Pl. 87

Wardrobe.

C

London, Published Sept.ᵗ 1ˢᵗ 1787, by I. & J. Taylor, N.º 56, High Holborn.

Pl. 88

Wardrobe.

D

Pl. 89

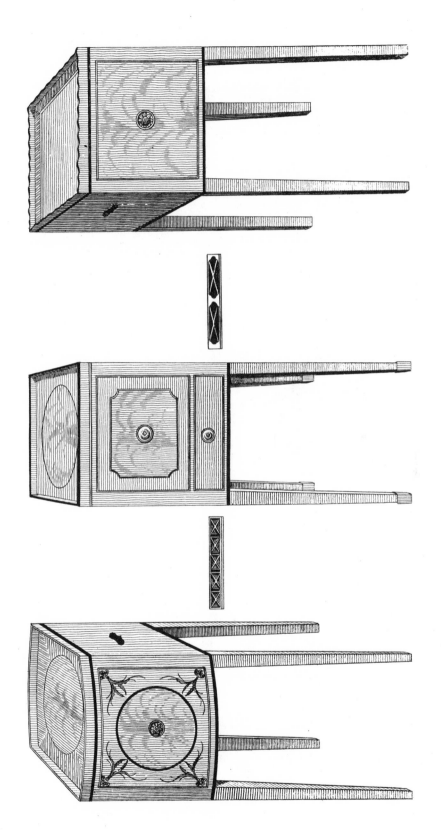

Pot Cupboards.

London, Published Sept.r 1.st 1787. by t & J. Taylor, No. 56, High Holborn.

Pl.90

Brackets. A.

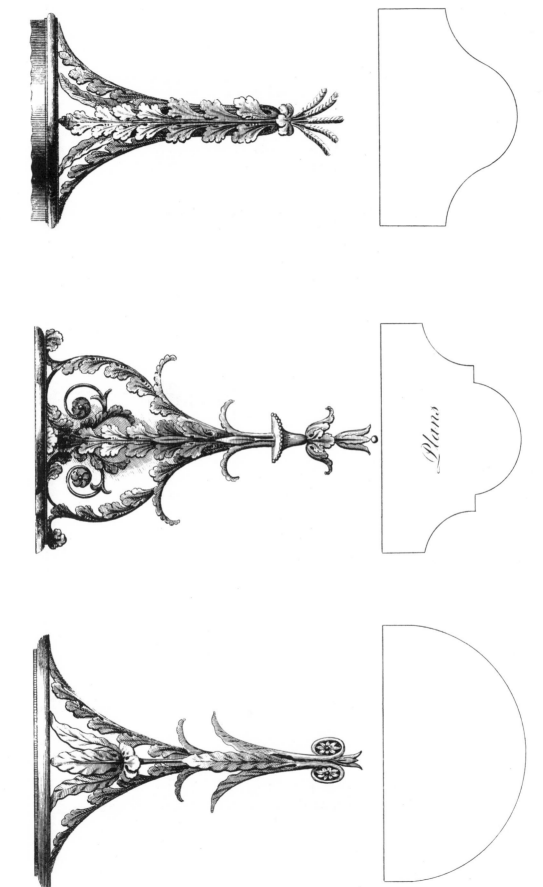

Plans

London, Published Sep.r 1.st 1787, by I.&J. Taylor, N.o 56. High Holborn.

Pl. 91

Brackets. B.

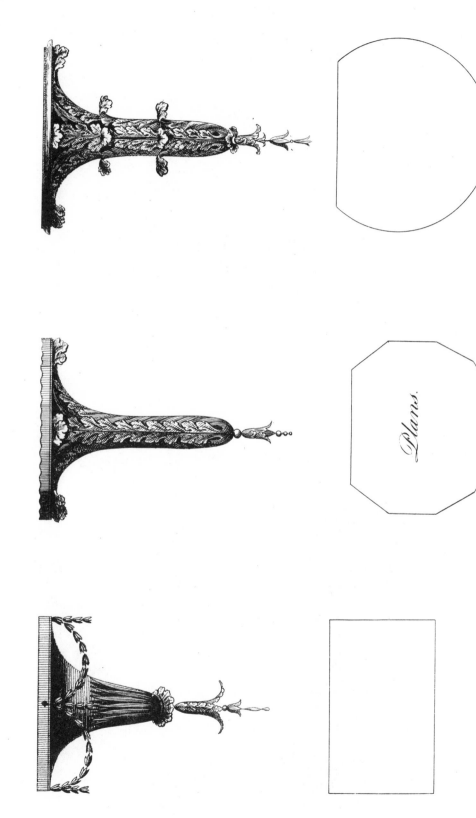

Plans.

London. Published Oct.r 1.st 1787. by I.&I. Taylor. N.o 56. High Holborn.

Pl. 92

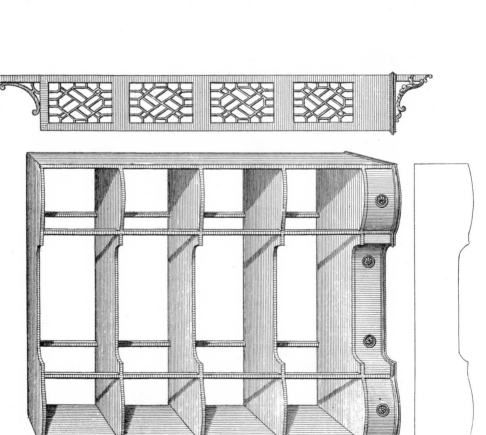

Hanging Shelves.

London Published Sept. 1st 1787. by I.& J.Taylor. No.56. High Holborn.

Pl.93

Pole Fire   Screens.

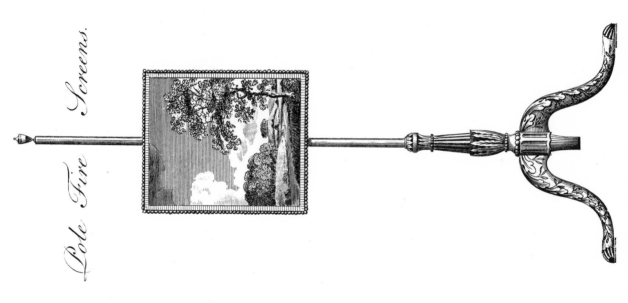

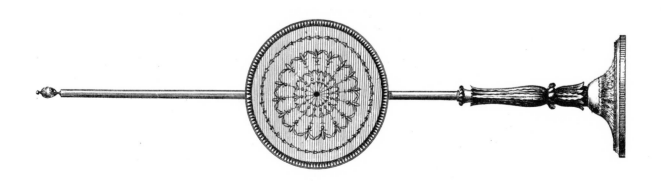

London, Published Oct.r 1.st 1787, by I.& J.Taylor, N.o 5 6, High Holborn.

Pl. 94.

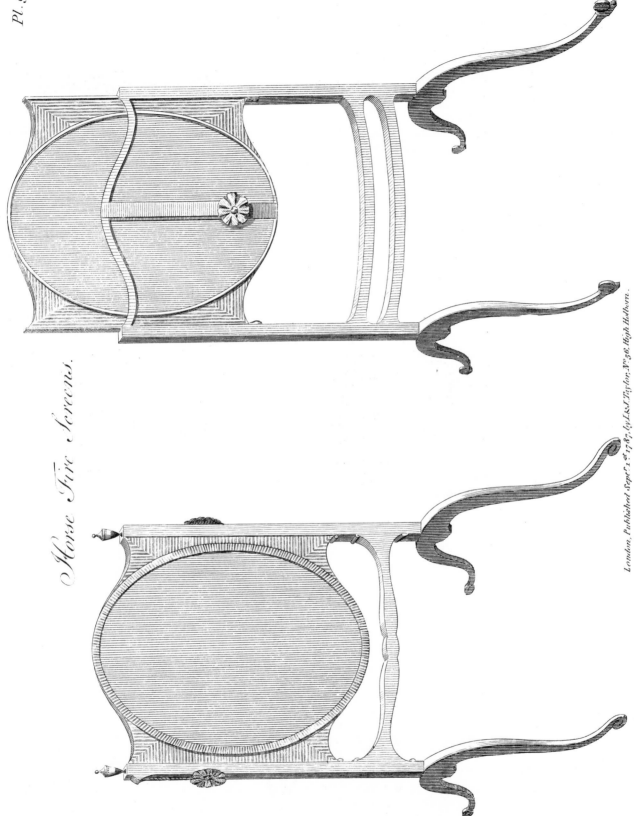

Horse Fire Screens.

London, Published Sept.r 1.st 1787, by I. & J. Taylor, N.º 56, High Holborn.

Pl. 95.

Design for a Bed.

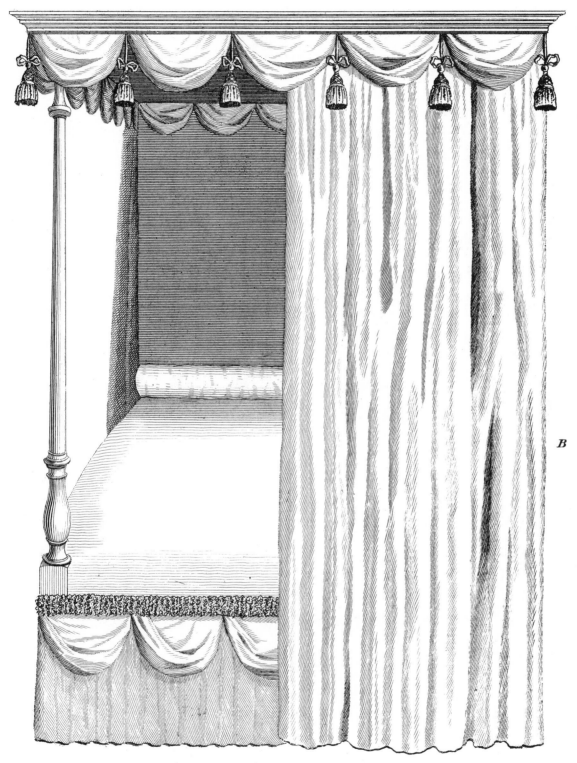

B

London, Published July 2ᵈ, 1787, by I.& J.Taylor, Nº 56, High Holborn.

Pl. 96

Design for a Bed.

London, Published Oct.r 1.st 1787, by I. & J. Taylor, No. 56, High Holborn.

Pl. 97

Design for a Bed.

London, Published Oct.r 1.st 1787, by I. & J. Taylor, No. 56. High Holborn.

A

London Published July 2ᵈ, 1787, by I. & J. Taylor, Nº 56, High Holborn.

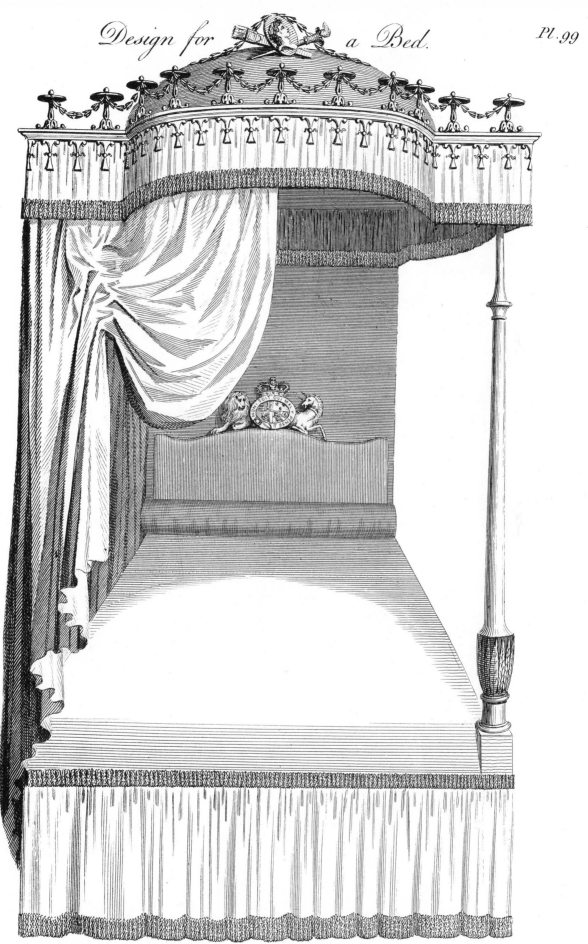

London, Published Oct.ʳ 1ˢᵗ 1787, by I. & J. Taylor, Nº 56, High Holborn.

Pl. 100

Design for a Bed.

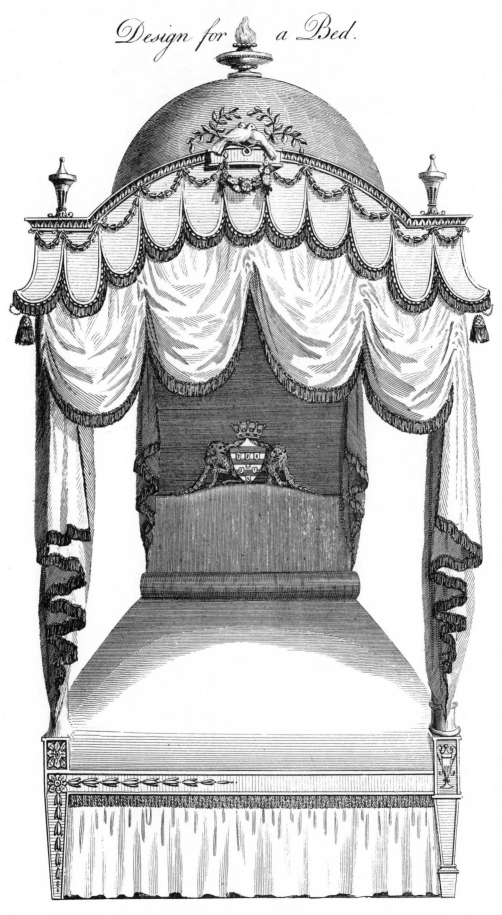

London, Published Oct.ʳ 1.ˢᵗ 1787, by I. & J. Taylor, N.º 56, High Holborn.

Pl. 101

Design for a Bed.

London, Published Oct.r 1.st 1787, by I. & J. Taylor, N.o 56, High Holborn.

Pl. 102.

Field Bed.

London, Published Oct.r 1st 1787, by I. & J. Taylor, No 56, High Holborn.

Pl. 103

Field Bed.

London, Published Oct.ʳ 1.ˢᵗ 1787, by I. & J. Taylor, N.º 56, High Holborn.

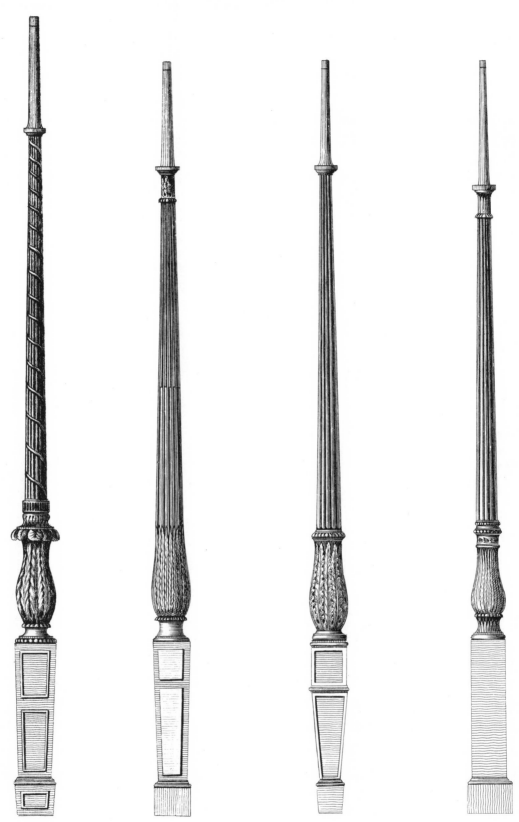

Pl. 106

Bed Pillars.

London, Published by I.&J. Taylor, Nᵒ 56, High Holborn, July 2ᵈ, 1787.

Pl. 107

Cornices for Beds or Windows.

A

B

C

London, Published July 2ᵈ 1787, by I.&J. Taylor, Nº 56, High Holborn.

Pl. 108

Cornices for Beds or Windows.

London, Published July 2, 1787, by I.& J. Taylor, Nº 56, High Holborn.

Pl.109

Cornices for *Beds or Windows.*

G

H

I

London, Published July 2, 1787, by I.& J.Taylor, No.56. High Holborn.

Pl. 110

Candle Stands.

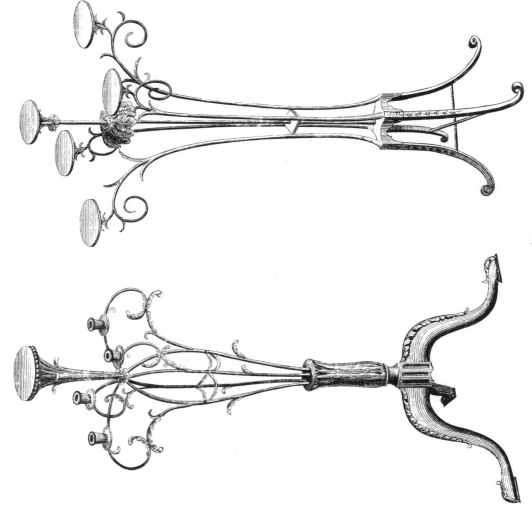

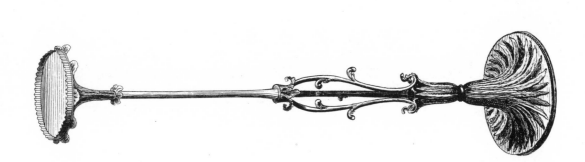

London, Published by I.&J.Taylor, No.56. High Holborn, July 2,1787.

Pl. III.

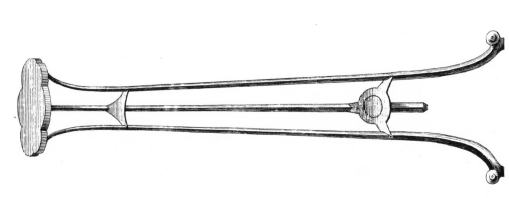

Candle Stands.

London, Published July 2ᵈ, 1787, by I.&J. Taylor, Nº 56, High Holborn.

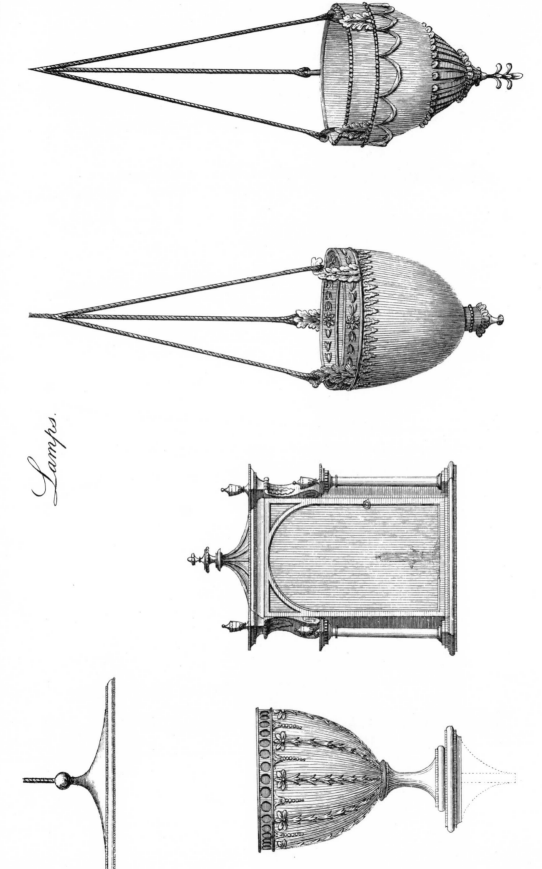

Pl. 112

Lamps.

London, Published Sept. 1.st 1787. by I.& J. Taylor, N.º 56 High Holborn.

Pl. 113

Girandoles.

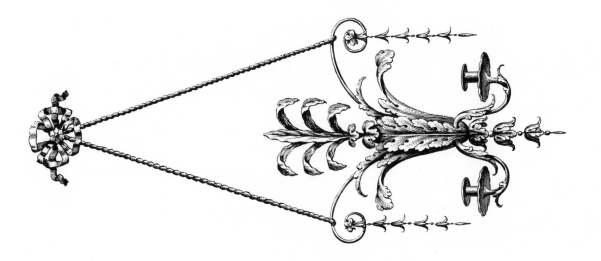

London, Published Sept.r 1.st 1787, by I.& J. Taylor, N.o 56, High Holborn.

Pl. 114

Girandoles.

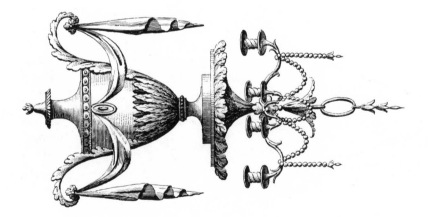

London, Published Sept.r 1.st 1787, by I. & J. Taylor, N.o 56, High Holborn.

Pl. 115

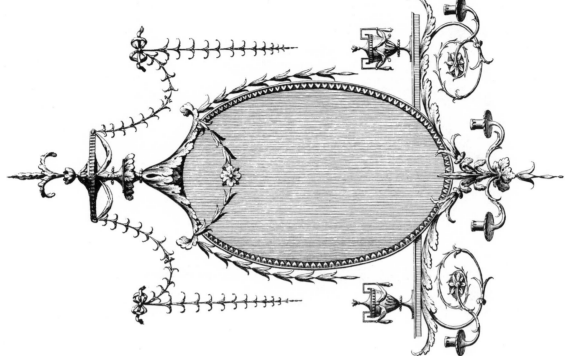

Girandoles.

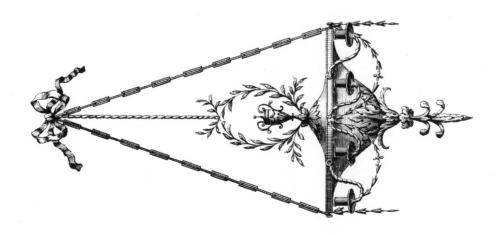

London, Published Sept.r 1.st 1787 by I.&.J. Taylor, N.o 56. High Holborn.

Pl. 116

Pier Glasses.

London, Published Sep.r 1.st 1787, by I. & J. Taylor, N.o 56. High Holborn .

Pl. 117

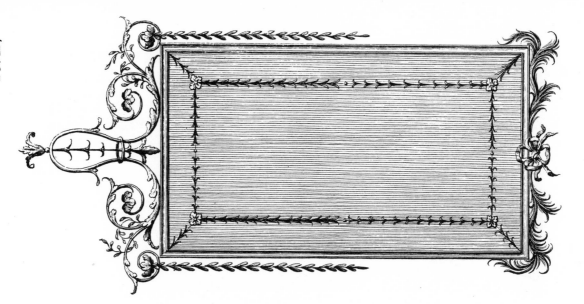

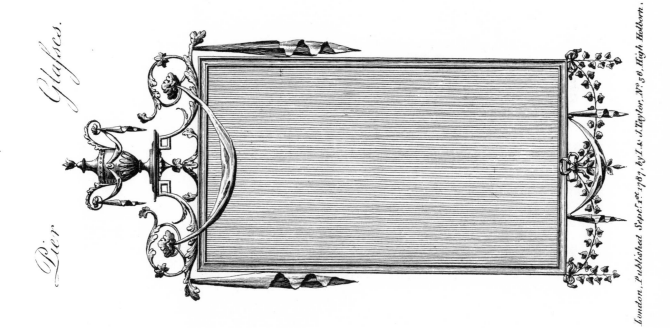

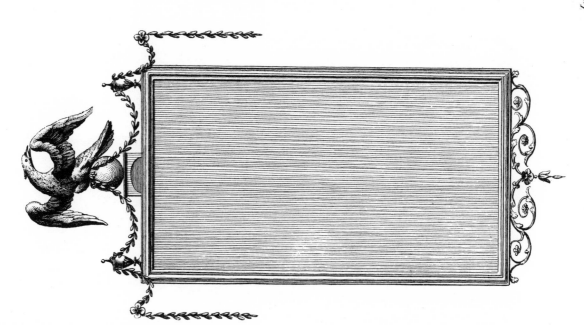

London, Published Sept.r 1.st 1787, by I. & J. Taylor, N.o 56. High Holborn.

Pl. 118

Glasses.

Pier.

London, Published Sept.r 1.st 1787, by I.& J. Taylor, N.o 56. High Holborn.

Pl. 119

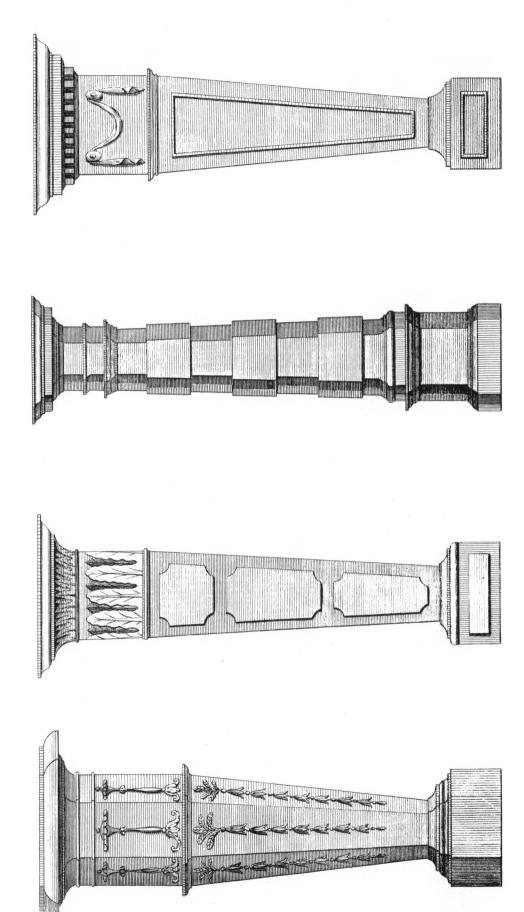

Terms for Busts, &c.

London, Published July 2, 1787, by I.&J. Taylor, N.° 56, High Holborn.

Pl.120

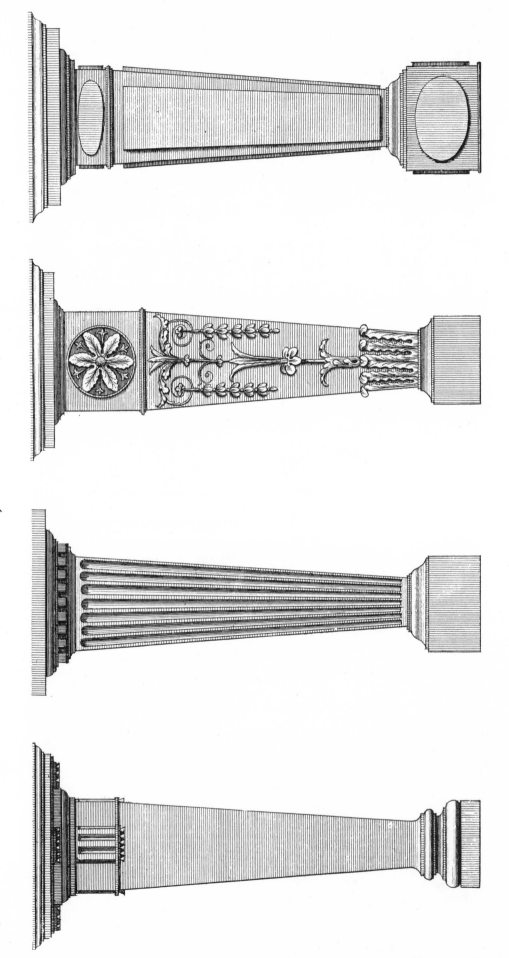

Terms for Busts, &c.

London, Published July 2, 1787, by I.&J.Taylor, N°.56, High Holborn.

1   2   3   4   5 Inches

London, Published Oct.r 1.st 1787, by I. & J. Taylor, No. 56, High Holborn.

Base Mouldings at large.

London, Published Oct.r 1.st 1787. by I. & J. Taylor, N.o 56, High Holborn.

1   2   3   4   5 Inches

London, Published Oct.ᵗ 1.ˢᵗ 1787, by I.&J.Taylor, Nᵒ 56, High Holborn.

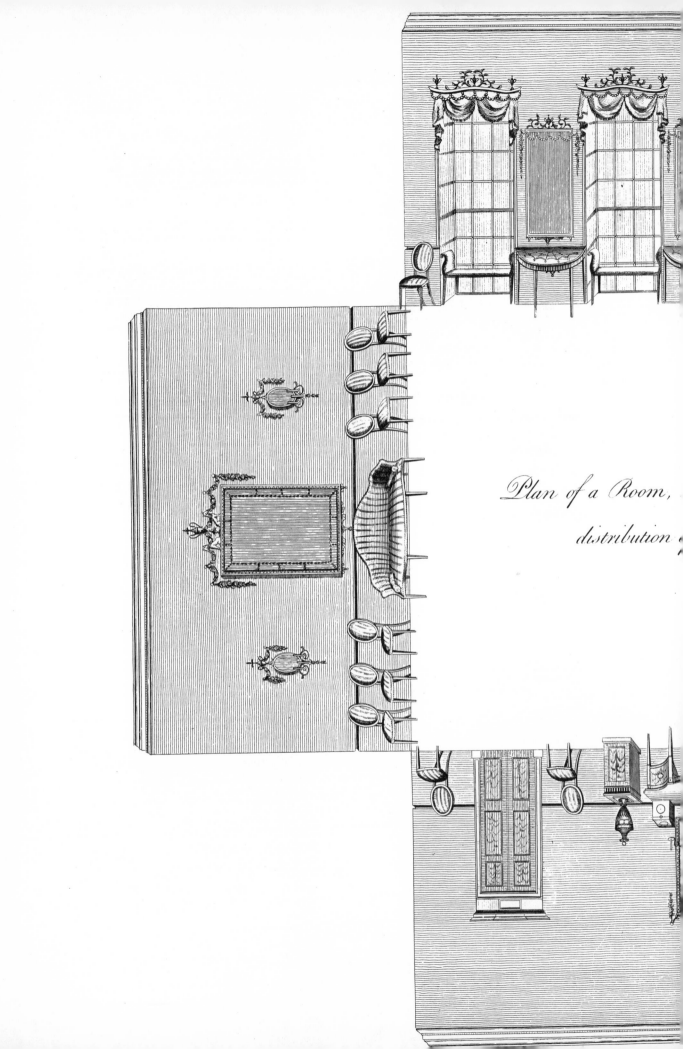

Plan of a Room,

distribution

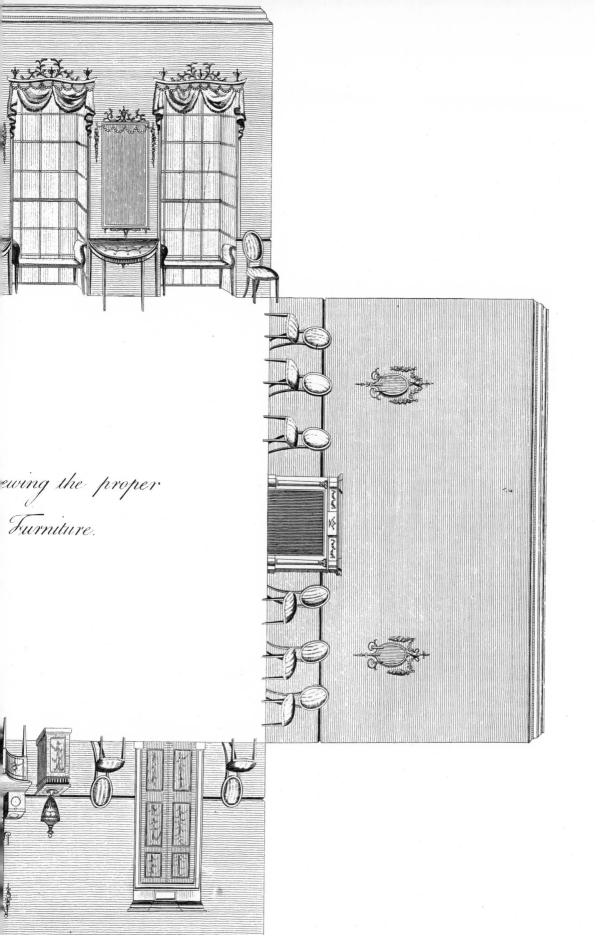

ewing the proper

Furniture.